The Gifts We Receive from Animals

The Gifts We Receive from Animals is a book guaranteed to brighten a reader's day. Professionals engaged in therapy work as well as those who have companion animals at home will enjoy learning about the many ways in which animals impact people's lives. Through a series of short, true-life stories, written by professionals engaged in animal-assisted interventions, *The Gifts We Receive from Animals* reminds readers of the core essence of the human-animal bond and the reason behind the growing phenomenon of animal-assisted interventions. Readers will learn, for example, about the young child who shares her inner most thoughts with a dog and, as a result, learns how to talk with people; the soldier who feels comfortable and safe with a dog, a feeling he has been lacking since active duty; and the elderly adult who works through difficult physical therapy because of his therapy dog. *The Gifts We Receive from Animals* takes readers on a delightful journey, offering insights into the unique impact animals have in the lives of those they help.

Lori R. Kogan, PhD, is a professor of clinical sciences at Colorado State University. She has published numerous journal articles and edited several books related to human-animal interactions.

Routledge Focus on Mental Health

Routledge Focus on Mental Health presents short books on current topics, linking in with cutting-edge research and practice.

For a full list of titles in this series, please visit www.routledge.com/Routledge-Focus-on-Mental-Health/book-series/RFMH

Titles in the series:

Transforming Performance Anxiety Treatment: Using Cognitive Hypnotherapy and EMDR
Elizabeth Brooker

The Relevance of Rational Emotive Behaviour Therapy for Modern CBT and Psychotherapy
Windy Dryden

An Evidence-based Approach to Authentic Leadership Development
Tony Fusco

Rational Emotive Behaviour Therapy: A Newcomer's Guide
Walter J. Matweychuk and Windy Dryden

Working with Interpreters in Psychological Therapy: The Right to be Understood
Jude Boyles and Nathalie Talbot

Psychoanalysis and Euripides' Suppliant Women: A Tragic Reading of Politics
Sotiris Manolopoulos

The Gifts We Receive from Animals: Stories to Warm the Heart
Lori R. Kogan

The Gifts We Receive from Animals

Stories to Warm the Heart

Edited by Lori R. Kogan

Routledge
Taylor & Francis Group

NEW YORK AND LONDON

First published 2023
by Routledge
605 Third Avenue, New York, NY 10158

and by Routledge
4 Park Square, Milton Park, Abingdon, Oxon, OX14 4RN

Routledge is an imprint of the Taylor & Francis Group, an informa business

© 2023 selection and editorial matter, Lori R. Kogan; individual chapters, the contributors

Library of Congress Cataloging-in-Publication Data
A catalog record for this title has been requested

ISBN: 978-1-03-206837-4 (hbk)
ISBN: 978-1-03-233463-9 (pbk)
ISBN: 978-1-00-320453-4 (ebk)

DOI: 10.4324/9781003204534

Typeset in Times New Roman
by Newgen Publishing UK

Contents

About the Editor   xi
List of Contributors   xii
Preface   xxi

PART 1
Large Animals   1

1 Freedom   3
   HILARY ADAMS

2 A Children's Riding Lesson: How Therapeutic Riding
   Helped a Boy to Find His Voice   6
   ANNE M.C. BARNFIELD

3 The Sundance Center   9
   ERICA JEX GERGELY

4 My Mare, My Meditation Teacher   12
   EMILY KNITTER

5 Savannah and the Cowgirl Ms. B   15
   ARIEAHN MATAMONASA BENNETT

6 The Farm Was My Sun   17
   CAROL RATHMANN AND SABRINA SCHMIDT

7 When the Cute Factor Becomes Something More:
How a Mini Donkey Taught Me the Power of the
Human-Animal Bond   20
CHRISTINA CARR

8 Meet Roger, the Blind Sheep Helping Children Heal   23
BRENDA RYNDERS

PART 2
Small Animals   27

9 Guinea Pigs Are Great!   29
PATTI ANDERSON

10 The Bunnies Are In   32
JENNIFER A. COLEMAN

11 Wait – My Therapy Animal Is a ... Rat?   35
ANGELA K. FOURNIER

12 A Crystallized Connection   38
JULIE ANN NETTIFEE

13 Sullivan Anne: From Abandoned Rabbit to Beloved
Campus Pet Therapy Animal   40
CLARISSA M. PALMER

14 Can I Take *Chophie* Home? The Simple Joys of Having
Animal Co-Therapists   43
GEORGITTA VALIYAMATTAM

15 The Rabbit Who Knew No Rules   46
PATTI ANDERSON

16 Who *Are* You?   49
NIKI VETTEL

PART 3
Crisis 53

17 Boston in Coal City 55
JULIE BERECKIS

18 HOPE AACR Responds to Devastating Mudslide 57
BETTE CALDWELL

19 Providing Comfort to Flood Victims of Rural West Virginia 60
SHEILA CONSAUL

20 Magical Moments with Maggie 63
YVONNE EATON-STULL

21 Can Dogs Sense Stress? 66
SUSAN HERMAN

22 Challenging the Assumption of Who Needs Help 69
BATYA G. JAFFE

23 The Washington Navy Yard 72
NED W. POLAN

24 The Dog That Brought Hope and Brightness to a
Challenging Christmas Season 75
YAHAIRA SEGARRA-GONZÁLEZ

25 Sometimes Silver Linings Have Tails: Sandy Hook 77
HEATHER WHITE

PART 4
Unique Settings 79

26 Assessment and Therapeutic Advancement through
Human-Animal Interactions 81
EILEEN BONA

27 Charley the Bulldog and Her Visits with Incarcerated Youth   83
    TAYLOR CHASTAIN GRIFFIN

28 Jude and Letty   86
    SARAH DEERING

29 The Life of a Strong and Caring Therapy Dog in the
    Canadian Prairies   89
    COLLEEN ANNE DELL (WITH THE ASSISTANCE OF
    DAVID BROCK BATSTONE)

30 Animal Therapy in a Hospice Setting   92
    CARYN FRIEDLANDER

31 In Sickness and in Health: What Dogs Teach Us about
    Life and Death   95
    RACHEL HOGG

32 "Steven" and Shannon   98
    AMY R. JOHNSON AND MELISSA POTTS KUTCHEK

33 Comfort during Crisis   101
    ANGELA MOE

34 Regaining Memories with the Help of Jaime   104
    ANNA K.E. SCHNEIDER

PART 5
Children, Young Adults and College Students   107

35 The Gift of Comfort   109
    SUE BURLATSCHENKO

36 Beignet and the Class of 2021   111
    KATE DRESCHER

37 Teletherapy Dogs   114
    ADAM DUBERSTEIN

38 The Power of Prince William   117
    PATRICIA FLAHERTY-FISCHETTE

39 Mickey Mouse and Lyn   120
    TARA HARVEY-GROS

40 Compassion through Canines: A Boy and a Dog   123
    LAURA HEY AND MARY JO POWERS

41 I Can Listen Like Indy   126
    TERRI HLAVA

42 Aksel to the Rescue   129
    ELIZABETH A. LETSON

43 A Gentle Giant and an Anxious Teen   132
    JANE JENKINS

44 Therapy Dogs Help Adoption Succeed   135
    GARY P. COURNOYER

45 Leo Awakens to the World   137
    SHIRA SMILOVICI

PART 6
Adults   139

46 Jaeger's Gifts   141
    SHANNAN ANDERSON

47 The Whirlwind That Changed My Life...   144
    ÚRSULA ARAGUNDE-KOHL

48 My Therapy Dogs Saved My Life   147
    MEGAN C.W. BRIDGES

49 Miss Emmie: A Big "Braveheart" in a Tiny Package   150
    DONNA CLARKE

50 Being and Becoming: The Transformative Power and
    Resilience of Person-Canine Bonds   153
    CASSANDRA HANRAHAN

51 Pinella's Purpose   156
    TIANA KELLY

52 A Golden Tail of Inter-Generational Bonds   159
    PATRICK J. KIRNAN AND JEAN P. KIRNAN

53 You Are Here   162
    ELIZABETH LYNCH

54 *Humanimal* Connection in the Counseling Room:
    Where Lester the Dachshund Partner Weaves an
    Interspecies Bond   165
    EMMANUELLE FOURNIER CHOUINARD
    TRANSLATED BY MARIE TOUNISSOUX

    Index   168

About the Editor

Lori R. Kogan, PhD, is a professor of clinical sciences at Colorado State University. She is the chair of the Human-Animal Interaction (HAI) section of the American Psychological Association and editor of the *Human-Animal Interaction Bulletin*, an open-access, online publication supported by the American Psychological Association. She has published numerous journal articles and book chapters and co-edited books including *Pet Loss, Grief, and Therapeutic Interventions: Practitioners Navigating the Human-Animal Bond*, *Clinician's Guide to Treating Companion Animal Issues: Addressing Human-Animal Interaction*, and *Career Paths in Human-Animal Interaction for Social and Behavioral Scientists* and given invited presentations on topics related to HAIs in both psychology and veterinary medicine venues. She is currently engaged in several research projects pertaining to the intersection of the human-animal bond and veterinary medicine.

Contributors

Hilary Adams is theatre director, certified equine gestalt coach, and founder of Story and Horse, LLC. Story and Horse partners with creative practitioners to support their growth through 1-1 business and life coaching, workshops, the Story and Horse Podcast, and educational opportunities. We offer virtual and in-person sessions that include horses as co-coaches.

Patti Anderson has been a therapy animal educator at the university level, through her LLC and as a volunteer. She has been registered through the Pet Partners organization throughout the years with 12 guinea pigs, 2 rabbits, and 7 dogs.

Shannan Anderson has 21 years of experience as a certified therapeutic recreation specialist working with people with traumatic brain injuries, strokes, amputations, spinal cord injuries, dementia, and congenital disabilities. Currently she is treating our nation's heroes at a VA Hospital as a recreation therapist and the therapy dog coordinator.

Úrsula Aragunde-Kohl is a clinical psychologist and a faculty member at the Universidad Ana G. Mendez, Gurabo Campus. She has worked on diverse initiatives that include the first AAI graduate course in Puerto Rico: "Animal-Assisted Interventions in Health Settings", research about the human-animal bond in her country, and she founded the nonprofit Puerto Rico Alliance for Companion Animals, Inc. (PR Animals).

Anne M. C. Barnfield D.Phil., is Interim Academic Dean and an Associate Professor of Psychology at Brescia University College, living in London, Ontario, with her husband Richard and their cat, Chinthe. Anne's current research focus is on equine-assisted/facilitated activities for children and on treatment of anxiety and post-traumatic stress disorder (PTSD) in adults.

Arieahn Matamonasa Bennett is a licensed psychologist, EAP practitioner, researcher, and professor at DePaul University in Chicago.

Julie Bereckis, RN-BSN CPN TNS, KPA CT, is a pediatric ICU nurse who loves to share the joy of her dog with others. She has been a therapy partner with PAWsitive Therapy Troupe since 2007 and a crisis response partner since 2014 – bringing smiles and comfort to others.

Eileen Bona, MEd, is a registered psychologist in Canada who founded the Dreamcatcher Nature Assisted Therapy program in 2003. This program rescues farm animals and partners them with people with complex mental health issues, servicing about 120 people a week and offering a full certification in animal-assisted therapy in Canada in partnership with a college – the first program of its kind in English-speaking Canada.

Megan C.W. Bridges is an animal loving, multi-talented, substance abuse counselor who specializes in animal-assisted therapy. She has dedicated her life to loving those who are hardest to love.

Sue Burlatschenko graduated from the Ontario Veterinary College. She also holds a Diplomate Status (ABVP), a Master of Public Health, and owns/operates a mobile food animal veterinary practice.

Bette Caldwell, after retiring from a long career in education, joined HOPE Animal-Assisted Crisis Response in 2015. Since then, she has been involved in approximately 75 deployments.

Emmanuelle Fournier Chouinard is a clinical psychologist working in animal-facilitated psychotherapy (child, adult, family), a teacher and supervisor in AAI (private and public settings, in Québec and France), a canine consultant, and the Director of *Centre Humanimal.*

Donna Clarke is a licensed clinical professional counselor (LCPC) currently working in private practice. She is a Board-Certified Telemental Health Provider (BC-TMH), nationally certified counselor (NCC), trained as a Certified Clinical Trauma Professional: Level 2 (CCTP-II), as well as Certified Grief Informed Professional (CGP). With more than twenty years involvement in animal rescue and welfare, Ms Clarke also holds a certificate in Animal-Assisted Therapy.

Jennifer A. Coleman is an assistant professor in the Department of Psychiatry and Behavioral Sciences at Rush University Medical Center and a clinical psychologist and the assistant director of Rush's Road Home Program, a nonprofit that provides no-cost mental health services for veterans and their family members. Her professional interests include trauma studies, HAI, health disparities, and group therapy.

Sheila Consaul has spent over 15 years providing pet therapy and animal-assisted crisis response for a variety of organizations throughout the metropolitan Washington, DC area. When she is not generating smiles and hugs with her golden retriever, Lucy, Sheila works as a communications and marketing consultant and lives in northern Virginia.

Gary P. Cournoyer, who worked in Juvenile Corrections for the majority of his time in state service, chose to go into private practice upon retirement. Due to the overwhelming number of children in the child welfare system who had experienced trauma, Mr. Cournoyer chose to specialize in this field and continued to work with his therapy dogs as he did in the Juvenile Correctional setting.

Sarah Deering is a mental health advocate and proponent for the human-animal bond. She has spent over a decade developing a unique approach to working with humans to find healing alongside our pets and founded Working Together Pet Programs LLC in Denver, CO.

Colleen Anne Dell is a professor and centennial enhancement chair in One Health and Wellness at the University of Saskatchewan in the Department of Sociology and School of Public Health in Canada. Grounded in a community-based, patient-centered participatory approach, her research focuses on healing from addictions and mental health, with specific attention to Indigenous populations and AAI (ranging from canine-assisted therapy through to service dog interventions).

Kate Drescher is a licensed clinical psychologist who has been working in a school setting with children and families for 16 years. In 2019 she was matched with a pure-bred golden retriever (service dog) named Beignet who serves as her therapeutic partner at school.

Adam Duberstein is an adjunct professor of psychology at Southern New Hampshire University. He is also employed full-time in clinical psychology practice in his hometown of Hazel Park, MI.

Yvonne Eaton-Stull is an associate professor of Social Work at Slippery Rock University of Pennsylvania. She has had five therapy dogs that she has worked with over the years providing animal-assisted therapy and animal-assisted crisis response.

Patricia Flaherty-Fischette is an AAI researcher, teacher, runner, mom, and clinical social worker, and resides in the suburbs of Philadelphia with her husband, two children, and rescue-dog, Ella. She is the Clinical Director of an organization supporting young adults with intellectual disabilities, the Research Fellow for SoulPaws Recovery Project, the only outpatient Animal-Assisted Activity program for individuals struggling food and body image issues, and Research Associate/Lecturer at Bryn Mawr College Graduate School of Social Work and Social Research.

Angela K. Fournier has a PhD in clinical psychology from Virginia Tech and is a licensed psychologist in Minnesota. As a professor in the Department of Psychology at Bemidji State University, she is the Director of the Humanimal Interaction Laboratory.

Caryn Friedlander, M.A, M.F.A., is a visual artist who lives and works in Bellingham, Washington. After volunteering in end-of-life care for ten years, she became a registered Pet Partners team handler with her golden doodle Tashi, and introduced the idea of using therapy animals at her local in-patient hospice. She and Tashi have served at Whatcom Hospice House for four years. She also volunteers with Friends for Life Animal Rescue, raising neonate orphaned kittens.

Erica Jex Gergely, PhD, is a licensed clinical psychologist with over 15 years of experience spanning clinical, research, teaching, and consulting fields. She is also certified in psychotherapy and learning incorporating horses. She practices and resides in Indianapolis, Indiana.

Taylor Chastain Griffin is the National Director of Animal-Assisted Interventions (AAI) Advancement at Pet Partners. In this role, she oversees the organizations' empirical research collaborations and works with other field leaders to motivate standardization and pro-fessionalization of the intervention.

Cassandra Hanrahan is an Associate Professor at the School of Social Work, Faculty of Health, Dalhousie University, Nova Scotia, Canada. Cassandra's research on animal-assisted interventions and animal-informed social work urges us to reconceptualize the purpose and practice of social work-incorporating the more-than-human world and to making sustainability a core value. By raising awareness of anthropocentrism and the prescience of a critique of humanism in social work, Cassandra advocates new ontologies of being and becoming.

Tara Harvey-Gros is an occupational therapist and is board certified in pediatrics. She incorporates registered therapy dogs into many of her therapy sessions.

Susan Herman has been doing therapy dog work since 1992 and has been a member of HOPE Animal-Assisted Crisis Response since 2015. She currently does therapy visits and crisis work with her four Leonbergers; Lilly, Talon, Mira, and Jessie.

Laura Hey has a BS in Occupational Therapy and is a certified Animal Assisted Intervention (AAI) specialist. She founded Health Heelers, Inc., in 2005 to create programs that offer exceptional Human Animal Interactions (HAIs) to enrich the quality of both the human and non-human participants' lives. She is also an adjunct instructor of Animal-Assisted Interventions at Carroll University in WI.

Terri Hlava is currently the personal human to Copper and Shay Hlava, and co-founder of H.A.B.I.T.A.T. (Human Animal Bond In Teaching And Therapies). She loves working with dogs and children, her teammates, and teaching Disabilities Studies and Justice Studies at Arizona State University.

Rachel Hogg is an Australian academic with a PhD in Equestrian Psychology and a research background in HAI, horse-human relationships, and animal-assisted therapies. Her work addresses the theoretical intersections between critical psychology, ecopsychology, gender studies, and animal lives.

Batya G. Jaffe, PhD, is an animal-assisted therapist and the Head of the Psychotrauma K-9 Unit of United Hatzalah of Israel. Batya is also an adjunct professor at the Wurzweiler School of Social Work at Yeshiva University.

Jane Jenkins, PhD, MA is a licensed psychologist who researched the effectiveness of equine facilitated psychotherapy as her doctoral focus. In addition to her current role as a psychologist for students in the veterinary medicine field, she owns and operates a small private practice. Jane is also a facilitator for the Veterinary Mental Health Initiative, a non-profit group providing mental health support for veterinarians. Horses have played a major role both over her lifespan and now in her career, and her future plans include integrating farm-based interventions into mental health services.

Amy R. Johnson, EdD, MA, MAT, LPC, CPDT-KA, UW-AAB, is a licensed professional counselor and dog trainer. She developed and directed Oakland University's online Center for Human Animal

Interventions for more than a decade. Additionally, she founded and directs the non-profit, Teacher's Pet: Dogs and Kids Learning Together, which pairs adjudicated youth with hard-to-adopt shelter dogs for the benefit of both. She has published several journal articles and book chapters as well as presented internationally on the topic of HAI and AAI.

Tiana Kelly is a licensed professional counselor who is also pursuing a certificate of education in animal-assisted psychotherapy and a doctoral degree in prevention science. In addition to spending time with her dog, Pinella, she enjoys volunteering with Susquehanna Service Dogs and Not One More Vet.

Jean P. Kirnan is a college professor teaching undergraduate psychology courses and conducting research in applied psychology, measurement, and HAI. She is also a therapy dog volunteer.

Patrick J. Kirnan works in health and wellness. He is also a therapy dog volunteer.

Emily Knitter is a counseling psychology PhD student and US Army veteran. Horses have played a major role both in her personal and professional growths. Her goal is to interweave their healing power into work with military veterans after graduation.

Melissa Potts Kutchek is an integrative health strategist with a deep passion for animal-assisted therapy. Gratefully she has been a facilitator and board member for Teachers Pet: Dogs and Kids Learning Together for over 4 years, mentoring at-risk youth, and teaching them to train shelter dogs so they become more adoptable and placed into their forever homes.

Elizabeth A. Letson, Founder of Eagle Vista Ranch & Wellness Center, holds an MS in Counseling Psychology and is a licensed professional clinical counselor practicing in Bemidji, MN. Having grown up with many four-legged friends, Liz has experienced firsthand the honest, direct communication, and support they offer people coping with life's challenges and is honored to be able to bring the same support to her clients.

Elizabeth Lynch is an avian veterinarian with a BA degree in Biology with a concentration in Neuroscience and Animal Behavior from Cornell University. She is a registered handler of multiple species with over 20 years of experience offering AAI. She is a National Program Educator and Evaluator for Pet Partners.

Angela Moe specializes in victimization, trauma, and healing at Western Michigan University, Department of Sociology. For the past four years she has worked alongside her canine companion, Sunny the Therapy Dog, in countless settings, particularly involving children who were abused and neglected.

Christina Carr is a Licensed Master Social Worker (LMSW), currently integrating her work with the human and animal bond in grief work, both addressing human-animal bonds in human loss and making space for animal-related grief. Christina has practiced AAI with a variety of species and will always cherish the privilege of working with miniature donkeys.

Julie Ann Nettifee, RVT, MS, VTS (Neurology), currently works for North Carolina State University-College of Veterinary Medicine, Department of Clinical Sciences. She holds an AAS in Animal Health Technology from the University of Minnesota-Waseca, a BS from the University of Wisconsin-Madison, and an MS from North Carolina State University. She has presented and published many articles nationally and internationally. Her interests include enhancing the human-animal bond through veterinary medicine, animal-assisted therapies, and long-term care.

Clarissa M. Palmer is a professor of education at Plymouth State University in New Hampshire where she teaches research design, assessment, and HAI courses. Her research focuses on the influence of companion animals on adolescent development specifically on college campuses and in restorative justice programming.

Ned W. Polan, PhD, retired vice president for global research and development for a major chemical company, is New England Coordinator for HOPE Animal-Assisted Crisis Response. In addition to crisis response, his golden retrievers Brinkley, Meg, and Piper make 200 visits annually to a hospital behavioral health facility, a rehabilitation center, a crisis stabilization facility, a VA soldiers' home, and college midterm and final exam stress relief days.

Mary Jo Powers is a thirty-five year career educator with a BA in Education and an MS in Guidance and Counseling. She's always believed in the healing power of animals. After working with the Health Heelers program with her students, she had personal experience and proof in the ability of animals (dogs in these instances) to make life-changing interventions with humans of all ages.

Carol Rathmann is the Founder and Director of Forget Me Not Children's Services created in 1992. The farm offers animal-assisted and horticultural therapeutic activities for child victims of abuse and neglect. The farm serves a variety of social service agencies that bring groups of children to the farm weekly for hour-long sessions and individuals for one-on-one mentoring. Carol is responsible for developing the farm's best practice model for animal-assisted therapeutic interventions.

Brenda Rynders, since her work with Charlie's Acres, has developed her own microsanctuary for rescued sheep called Sheepy Hollow Sanctuary – where love, compassion, and Halloween cheer last 365 days a year. Brenda possesses master's degrees in Clinical Psychology and Anthrozoology and continues to promote inner healing and wellness through AAI.

Sabrina Schmidt received services at Forget Me Not Farm for over 10 years. As an adult she returned to volunteer at the farm and became a kitten foster parent at the local Humane Society. She is employed full time as a driver for disabled adults in Sonoma County. She lives in Santa Rosa with her rescued cat Ivy.

Anna K.E. Schneider works as a research fellow in the interdisciplinary study program Standards of Decision-Making Across Cultures. One of her research axes in sociology focuses on multispecies studies with a special interest in interspecies interaction.

Yahaira Segarra-González is a counseling psychologist who works as an assistant director and associate professor of the counseling psychology graduate program at Albizu University. She teaches and conducts research pertaining to the human-animal bond and has previous experience in animal-assisted psychotherapy with two registered therapy dogs named Astro and Pecas.

Shira Smilovici, PsyD, was born in the United States and raised in Mexico City (where she still resides). She has been an animal-assisted psychoanalytic psychotherapist since 2013. She has four passions in her life: her family, psychoanalysis, animals, and teaching.

Georgitta Valiyamattam received her doctorate as a Fulbright scholar at the Center for the Human-Animal Bond at Purdue. She is currently an assistant professor at Gitam University, India, where her research examines the benefits of animals for children with developmental conditions.

Niki Vettel, MA, MEd, is a registered Pet Partners® team handler and was pet mom to the first registered pet therapy guinea pig in Massachusetts. She has worked as a group therapist with a wide range of patient populations in hospital PHP programs, and incorporates animal-assisted therapy in groups focusing on mindfulness and trust. She lives in Winthrop with guinea pigs Calvin and Hermie, and rescue cat Kizzie (who doesn't bother the cavies!).

Heather White, LMSW, is a mental health practitioner in New York State and owner of Human-Animal Interactions company, AIM HAI, LLC. Heather is a Doctor of Social Work student at the University at Buffalo.

Preface

The Power of the Bond

"WHO'S THERE?", yelled Lonnie, a slightly built, stooping man – a long-term resident at the nursing home I visited as a psychology graduate student. "GET OUT!", he followed, standing in the middle of his small room, quickly becoming increasingly agitated. "I SAID GET OUT, GET OUT!" he snapped again, just in case I didn't quite understand what he meant. I paused near the door and then withdrew quietly; defeated. I knew not to take Lonnie's response personally, I had been warned that Lonnie yelled at everyone, but still, I had hoped I could somehow make it different.

"Oh, you are the student intern? OK, you can try and visit Lonnie, but don't say we didn't warn you. He doesn't talk to anyone". They explained that Lonnie yelled at everyone and never let anyone into his room. You see, Lonnie was blind, hard of hearing and had limited cognitive abilities. The staff had a very difficult time interacting with Lonnie and as a result, he spent nearly all his time alone, sitting in his bland room with the TV blaring, unable to see the screen. Yet, I was drawn to Lonnie; I saw the scared boy/man he was and wanted to find a way to connect. I saw a lonely man who spent every day alone, with no stimulation or social contact, and it broke my heart. So, every week, I would try again. I would knock loudly at his door and announce who I was before I entered. Week after week, I was firmly (and loudly) told to get out. I was not sure what else to try until one day I happened upon the facility's resident rabbit, a large grey delightful Holland Lop named Sam. The nursing home's social worker brought Sam to work each day and included him in some of her resident interactions. Not only was Sam the cuddliest bunny I had met, but as I came to learn, he was extremely patient and loved to sit on a warm lap and enjoy the attention he received. It was clear he enjoyed his job and was much loved by the staff and residents alike. I figured it couldn't hurt; perhaps, I could try and visit Lonnie with Sam.

On my next trip to the nursing home, I picked up Sam on my way to Lonnie's room. When I was greeted with the usual "WHO'S THERE, GET OUT!", I answered, "Lori, and I brought Sam, the bunny". Silence. "A bunny?" Lonnie asked quietly. (I had never heard Lonnie use a quiet voice before, this was a welcome change!)

"Yes, a bunny. Do you want to pet him?" I came closer to Lonnie and helped him sit on the edge of his bed (the only furniture in his room since he had no visitors) so I could sit beside him with Sam in my lap. I took Lonnie's hand and gently placed it on Sam's upper back. With the most tender of touches, Lonnie stroked Sam's back. Timidly, quietly, Lonnie said, "He is really soft". "Yes, he is, and he really likes how you are petting him". I replied. And so we sat like that, quiet, not talking, but connecting, both of us petting Sam. And Lonnie's world shifted ever so slightly.

From that day forward, each week, I would make sure I picked up Sam on my way to Lonnie's room and when I responded to the gruff "WHO'S THERE" with "It's me, Lori, with Sam", I was greeted with a rare smile. He would eagerly allow me to guide him to the bed so that he could enjoy time petting Sam. The fact that this was the only type of physical touch that Lonnie experienced made these moments even more precious. Because Lonnie's defense to his fears was anger, no one tried to approach him anymore, let alone hold his hand or give him an occasional hug. He had no family, no visitors; it had likely been years since Lonnie had let someone into his sensory-limited world. Yet, I had found the magic key, it was Sam. After that, our visits consisted of Lonnie and I, sitting on his bed, talking and petting Sam. We talked about his fears of getting a roommate or being forced to move to another room (a terrifying thought for a blind man who needed to feel some sense of control). We talked about memories he enjoyed as a child. I began bringing books to read to him and he would sit and listen while stroking Sam.

After one visit in which I noticed Lonnie's forehead was bruised and swollen, and learned he often hit his head on the corners of his nightstand, I was able to put corner protectors on his furniture (the staff had tried but he had ripped them off). During another visit, I presented Lonnie with a "talking" watch that stated the time out loud. He allowed me to put it on his wrist and "played" the time numerous times each day. Lonnie became my favorite resident and I truly enjoyed our visits. All these transformations were only possible, however, because of Sam. Witnessing this transformation was one of my first exposures to the magic of human-animal interactions (HAI). I was hooked.

Fast forward a couple years to my first post-graduate position – one that included counseling university students. After settling in, I began bringing my certified dog, Damien – an adorable black cocker/dachshund mix (with ultrasoft fur and chubby, disproportionately short 3-inch legs) to work with me. One day while in my office, I was called to see if I could help with a quickly escalating crisis. It appeared that a young undergraduate student had crawled under a desk in a large lecture classroom and was screaming and sobbing hysterically. It was between class periods and efforts to move her out of the room so that the next class could enter had not been successful. Over a hundred students were waiting to enter the room and a handful of instructors were frantically trying to navigate the growing crisis. Quickly leaving my office, Damien beside me, I entered the classroom and, based on the cluster of worried-looking instructors and loud sobbing, I knew where to head. I walked over, knelt down by the crying young woman, introduced myself and explained that I was there to help. No response. I then mentioned that I had my dog with me. "You have a dog?" she asked, as she lifted her head from her arms just high enough to look around. "Yes, he is right here" I explained. She reached out her hand and Damien was more than happy to approach for a possible rub. As she began to pet him, her crying subsided. After a couple minutes, I asked her if she would like to come back to my office with Damien and I, and she nodded her head. I helped her crawl back out from under the desk, and the three of us made our way back to my office. As we were leaving, the students outside began filtering in to start their class. Crisis averted; Damien had saved the day.

I share these stories because they left a mark on me and solidified my path. I had long known how much my animals enrich my life, but now I had also witnessed firsthand the magic they can bestow on others. The power they have to reach across otherwise unsurmountable barriers, to forge connections. Treated with care and kindness, animals offer us so much. The field of HAI, and AAI in particular, is growing rapidly and consists of rich, diverse and expansive research. Research that validates what our hearts have long known. I am a researcher at heart and feel that solid HAI-related research is critical for the advancement of the field, and yet, at the same time, sometimes it is helpful to pause and remember the stories and memories that warm our hearts, the ones that drive us to this line of work. That is what "The Gifts We Receive from Animals" is – a collection of heartwarming, personal stories that connect us, that illuminate why we continue striving to make the world a bit brighter with the help of our furry companions. Enjoy.

Lori R. Kogan, PhD

Part 1
Large Animals

1 Freedom

Hilary Adams

Sometimes, when I'm working with a client, the hardest part is the letting go. Letting go of what is no longer needed, and what is holding the clients back from moving forward.

It was a lovely, late August afternoon when Cynthia and I met. It was warm, but not too warm, and the light filtered through an overhanging tree that gave us shelter and a feeling of security. We were at a small farm location, out away from the house, by the pasture. My horse co-coach, Ray, a tall, red-haired guy with a sweet, kind nature and special fondness for hugs and apples, was hanging out by the fence of the round pen, only a few feet from where we sat in our two folding chairs.

Cynthia had arrived certain that what we were looking at for this session was her schedule. It was packed, left no room for what she called "extras," and served everyone's needs but her own. One of her values, something that kept coming up each time we spoke, was the idea of freedom. Her schedule was the opposite of freedom. It was like she woke up in shackles every day.

Each time we circled near the challenge of the schedule though, she'd get all tense, her body would almost curl, and she'd inhale and not exhale for a good long time. It was clearly fear, but of what? She needed to stand up and physically embody the journey toward the origin point of this behavior.

So, as we do with equine gestalt work, I turned toward Ray and asked if he'd help us out. We'd already introduced the two of them early in the session, and Cynthia had no fear of horses and was eager to go into the round pen with him.

I asked her to go to the center and drop her energy into the ground and take some deep breathes. Ray, a coaching pro, went right over, ready to work. I then asked her to walk to the fence of the round pen. Ray

DOI: 10.4324/9781003204534-2

followed. They slowly walked a circle, which turned into a spiral. As she walked, she thought back to when she first remembered feeling this sense of being shackled to a schedule, this deep requirement of responsibility to others at the expense of her own well-being. Ray followed right alongside, supporting her each step, stopping when she stopped, and being there for her to put her hand on for reassurance.

As she arrived toward the center of the spiral, Ray turned his body around so that he was facing her head on, dropping his eyes down so that he was looking right at her. Cynthia stopped, met his gaze, and said, "You're right."

As the human coach, I had no idea what Ray was right about, and it did not matter. He was communicating with her, and she was somewhere else with him, in a landscape I was not inhabiting. She began to cry, and Ray stood without moving as she wrapped her arms around her neck, burying her face into him.

After a long moment, as she slowly stopped crying, she kept her hands on Ray and turned to include me in the discovery she'd made. "I was always taking care of my siblings," she said, running a hand along Ray's neck as he sighed with contentment.

> That was how I felt I mattered, how I felt loved. I didn't want to. I wanted to go out and play, do my things, but I couldn't. That would be selfish. And that's what I'm doing now. My schedule is little me desperately wanting love. My family loves me, and I love them. I don't need to schedule like this. *I can find a different way. I want to let this way go.*

This is the hardest moment for clients; it takes great courage, this letting go of the old to move into the new.

I joined them in the round pen, carrying a halter, lead rope, and saddle pad. I told her, I want you to put this saddle pad onto Ray, imagining it's this old form of scheduling, this old idea that, unless you took care of everyone, every minute of every day, you would not be loved, put all of that whole feeling into this pad and then onto Ray. He'll carry it away for you.

And that's what he did, this tall red horse, a wise coach with four hooves. I haltered Ray as she held the pad for a good long moment, before putting it carefully onto Ray's back.

Cynthia quietly said, "Thank you Ray, thank you."

Ray exhaled, and, without me asking, started to move, carrying the old away for her, seemly as eager to get rid of it as she was.

Cynthia, her voice trembling with excitement, called out after us as we left the round pen, "I'm free. *I'm free!*"

Discussion Questions:

1 How do you feel that Ray helped facilitate Cynthia's insight?
2 Explain why riding Ray was not necessary for Cynthia to benefit from his participation in the session.

2 A Children's Riding Lesson

How Therapeutic Riding Helped a Boy to Find His Voice

Anne M.C. Barnfield

A children's riding lesson: what comes to mind? Maybe children calling out to one another, giggling, chatting, making noise. You would probably think something like this because that is what most children would do. Most, but not all, however. For all human behavior there is a range, a continuum. Most people are somewhere in between the extremes of any measure; some, however, are at those extremes.

Among the issues characterized by the American Psychological Association (APA) as "neurodevelopmental disorders" are the Autism Spectrum Disorders (ASDs). Each person diagnosed with ASD is unique, with different symptoms and their own specific abilities. Because of the range of characteristics, this condition is named a "spectrum" disorder, whereby anyone can be at some point along a line, a spectrum.

Children with ASDs are good at perception (e.g., seeing details), but poorer at "theory of mind", the understanding of another's perspective. It is very difficult for a child with an ASD to see a situation from another's point of view. While understanding of others' thinking usually begins around age four in typically developing children, those diagnosed with an ASD have difficulty understanding the viewpoint of others. Imagine interacting with one who behaves this way, someone who doesn't understand that you may feel differently, see things differently – that you are a totally different person.

Even "high-functioning" children with ASDs have difficulties with the subtleties of social interaction and communication. It may seem far-fetched, particularly to those who do not often interact with or care for animals, but activities with animals such as riding lessons can have remarkable effects for children with ASDs.

One example of such effects is given by a boy whom I will call "Evan". Evan was a participant in a study on effectiveness of therapeutic riding (TR) for children. Through the TR sessions, I would watch

DOI: 10.4324/9781003204534-3

what went on, sitting quietly on the sidelines, noting specific behaviors and interactions.

When he started riding lessons, Evan was not calling out or making noise, he didn't giggle or chatter – on the contrary, he was quiet, withdrawn, and non- communicative. There was practically no social interaction seen in that first observation, just the odd "yes" or "no" in response to a direct question from the instructor. Even after ten weekly sessions, although Evan appeared a bit more engaged, he was still quite withdrawn. There was still little talking to, or interacting, with others in the group. Evan did interact more with the pony he was riding, however, patting its neck and quietly saying things like "good boy". One time the instructor questioned this, asking "Why did you say that?" Avoiding eye contact, Evan replied quietly but emphatically "he is!" All the ponies at the TR center are selected for steadiness, calmness, and good nature, and Toby, the dapple-grey pony which Evan had been assigned for his lessons, was no exception.

Near the end of another ten weeks of weekly sessions, a remarkable thing happened. Evan and another child, "Alex", were both riding their respective ponies. The instructor asked about trying a game, both children said "yes"; Evan with a single word answer, Alex enthusiastically saying "Yes, please!" What was astonishing was what happened next. The children had to take turns and the instructor asked: "Who'd like to go first?" Evan spoke up immediately, saying "You go first Alex, go on". Everyone present (instructor, parents, even me) held our breath as the instructor said: "You're OK with Alex going first?" "Yes", Evan replied, "That's alright, Alex can go first, he wants to". Not only had Evan responded, he'd responded with more than a single word answer and, most heartwarming, had thought of the other child and his wants, putting that other person first. Near end of the sessions, after 19 riding lessons, Evan answered questions and gave a full response including consideration of the other child in the lesson – amazing!

In an earlier study, a parent had told me about another child who had a hard time talking properly to people, talking "at" people, not "to" them. He explained that he had seen a lot of improvement in his child's interactions with other people and felt it was his son's interaction with the ponies that made the difference.

Here, I saw that happen myself. I realized that the special bond Evan had formed with Toby had worked its magic – it had helped Evan interact better with the people around him. His ability to connect with Toby translated into an increased ability to connect with others – truly representing the unique gifts that animals can offer to children like Evan.

Discussion Questions:

1   What about working with a service dog – how would you encourage
    interaction with a dog, to achieve a similar outcome?
2   How might we use this type of animal interaction to aid a child in a
    school classroom?

3 The Sundance Center

Erica Jex Gergely

Out in the pasture, I felt a sense of excitement and fear as I stood with the horses grazing freely. Until recently, I could count on one hand the number of times I'd even been *near* a horse, and now, here I was in their space – their world – up close and personal. I couldn't help but think, *how did I get here?*

I was twenty-seven years old and a hard-working clinical psychology graduate student looking for a creative outlet to de-stress. This search led me to taking beginner horseback riding lessons at a nearby hobby farm that provided more peacefulness and tranquility than I'd ever imagined possible. Sometimes I'd visit the horses, not to ride, but to simply *be* with them; it was calming and relaxing.

Being a graduate student with an eye toward research studies and my nose often buried in books, it didn't take long for me to begin formally exploring the connection between horses and humans. I wondered if the calming effect I felt while with horses was real. Was there any evidence of an actual horse-human bond? My brief search led me to the discovery of equine-assisted services, and I was eager to learn as much as I could.

Much to my surprise, I found a local psychologist who practiced equine-assisted therapy. After a brief conversation, she kindly invited me to her farm to participate in my own equine-assisted learning (EAL) session.

That's how I got here, at The Sundance Center.

That's how I found myself out in the pasture alongside the horses.

Now with the added task instructors invited me to try: "Choose a horse and lead it over the raised log".

The horses weren't haltered nor were there any ropes nearby. *How on earth will I get either horse to move? Is this a trick?* I thought silently.

After asking several clarifying questions, and receiving mostly non-committal answers, I reluctantly started. *Here goes nothing.*

DOI: 10.4324/9781003204534-4

The beauty of the red horse, Sydney, quickly drew me to her, and as I approached, she willingly stepped closer with a gentle curiosity, nuzzling, and nudging me with her nose. It seemed as if we connected almost instantaneously, and as her head draped over my shoulder, I could feel the trust building. With the task in mind, I decided to walk toward the log, and sure enough, she followed me! Over the log I hopped, and so did she – but almost immediately it fell. *I knew that was too good to be true.*

With Sydney still in tow, we circled back around to attempt again, this time picking up some speed. Three legs cleared the log before it came crashing down. *Fail.* For the next half hour, Sydney and I worked side by side to jump over the log, and when it would fall after each attempt, I'd become ever more discouraged at my failure.

Finally, I paused and sheepishly asked the onlooking instructors, "Are you sure she can do this?" They both shrugged and matter-of-factly replied, "Oh, we have no idea!"

I couldn't believe my ears. *It was a trick!*

"How's it going?" asked the facilitator.

"Terrible!" I shouted, "I've failed every time".

"Failed?" she questioned.

"Yeah, Sydney's knocked the log down every time. I don't know what I'm doing wrong".

"Did all four feet make it over the log?", she questioned.

"Only after the log was on the ground, so that doesn't count. That's not a success", I clarified.

"Did we say the log had to stay up on the supports?" *Hmmm.*

"Did we say you couldn't put the log on the ground?" *Double Hmmm.*

"I guess not", I answered as I reflected on their simple instructions: **Choose a horse and lead it over the raised log.** "Apparently I overcomplicated things and maybe set too high of expectations".

"Interesting", remarked the instructor as she stood and let me process.

Overcomplicate things. Set too high of expectations. I do this a lot, I thought.

"What went well?" she asked.

I'd been so caught up in my perceived failures that I hadn't mentioned all the wonderful, beautiful successes with Sydney. "So much! Our bond, our trust, our teamwork, our communication. Her persistence – she didn't give up, she continued, willingly, until I paused … what an incredible experience!" On and on I shared my thoughts.

Wow, how could I have learned so much, so quickly, from a horse?

That day changed my life. Not in a cliché sense, it truly opened new doors for me. I continued to learn about equine-assisted services and ultimately combined my love of horses with my graduate work for my doctoral dissertation.

Today, I offer EAL to individuals and groups looking to gain insights about themselves, their relationships, and the world around them. Through EAL I've had the pleasure of watching many people grow personally and professionally, and the honor of witnessing them receive unique gifts from their horse partners.

Discussion Questions:

1   In the story, the woman's perception of success vs. failure was challenged. Success looks different for everyone; we each must define what success looks like to us. What does success look like for you?

2   Sometimes people engage in unhelpful thinking styles, like "all-or-nothing thinking" where things are either really good/successful or really bad/failure and they don't consider anything in between. Do you ever think this way? What are the consequences of this thinking?

4 My Mare, My Meditation Teacher

Emily Knitter

The stall door groans as I use my shoulder to slide it open. My breath appears in a cloud before me. It is still freezing even in the barn, with warmth radiating off a dozen horses' bodies. It's a January evening in Western New York, so I can't expect much else. My mare, Star, is waiting for me. She sniffs my gloved hand in greeting, and I reach up to scratch her favorite spot behind the ear. Her soft, fluffy winter coat kicks up another cloud, this time of dust. The dust mixes with my breath and sparkles as it catches the final rays of sun through the barn window.

As I enter, Star takes a single step away from me, moving deeper into the stall. She sighs and drops her head even with my chest. Her eyes half closed; she cocks her hind hoof in relaxation. Her energy becomes distant, internal. Usually, she is antsy to leave her stall when I arrive. Is something wrong? I send a text to the barn owners asking if there were any differences in her routine today. Had she been playing hard in the field? No, nothing out of the ordinary.

Then I remember horses need a feeling of safety to sleep. They can go years with only small naps if they don't feel secure. Has the work I've been doing since purchasing Star a few months ago finally started to connect? I remind myself to breathe and go through my checklist of meditation techniques.

Breathe in four breaths. Hold four breaths. Out as slow as possible, minimum six breaths. Hold four breaths, repeat.

Once my energy begins to calm and slow, I shift my focus back to Star. I notice her ears angled out to the sides, relaxed, not held tense. Good. That indicates she is feeling relaxed and not retreating to a shut-down state inside her head. Her eyes are still halfway closed. This could mean she is processing a large amount of internal stress or she is super

DOI: 10.4324/9781003204534-5

relaxed. Using the other body language clues she is providing makes me believe it's the latter. Letting my gaze drift down to her muzzle, I see her nostrils are round and unwrinkled. Another clue she's not worried. I notice her lower lip twitching slightly. I've learned that's her sign she's about to take a deep breath and relax even further – if she remains uninterrupted. I keep a soft focus on her muzzle and tune back into my breathing.

In. Hold. Out. Hold.

Moments later, she releases a deep sigh and begins to lick and chew. I can't keep myself from grinning. She remains half asleep, and I send a mental image telling her she is safe, I will stand guard as long as she wants to rest. I tune back into my breathing.

In. Hold. Out. Hold.

Meditation has been something I can never seem to stick with. But to have the honor of using it to help Star? I've got this. Thoughts come and I visualize them drifting away like clouds. I then switch to a modified loving-kindness visualization technique. I imagine a warm light appearing above her, although it is now dark in the barn. I try to send her all the feelings of love I have and imagine the light growing in response, warming her.

It reminds me of how far we've come together in such a short time. Coming together, we both have had to learn how to communicate, to slow down, to breathe. As our familiarity has grown, my awareness has developed. That's why this moment is so precious. To have a glimpse of Star feeling seen and heard. Knowing she feels understood enough to allow me to protect her. I am honored. I come back into the moment and visualize those thoughts drifting off too.

In. Hold. Out. Hold.

Finally, letting out a deep breath, Star stretches her neck up and back and then looks at me like, what's next, mom? That must have been a solid twenty minutes. Pulling my phone from my pocket, I don't believe the time. I look again, to be extra sure. I shake my head. An hour and a half has passed.

I grin and scratch her favorite itchy spot behind the ear again. She is alert but calm. Ok girl, let's go to work. I lean my shoulder into the stall door once again, opening it wider. I slip the soft leather halter over her head, and we step out into the aisleway. Her metal shoes ring against the concrete. Our breath appears in the air and intertwines together as we walk toward the arena. It becomes impossible to tell hers from mine, and then the cloud drifts away.

Discussion Questions:

1   Meditation is predominantly taught as a solitary activity. Have you considered incorporating horses, or other animals, as a component? Why or why not?
2   The author describes the motivation to help her horse as the key to pursuing meditation for herself. How can we develop and use the human-animal connection as a therapeutic tool to meet individual treatment goals?
3   Have you ever considered utilizing animal relaxation as an intervention for a human? What are your thoughts after reading this story?

5 Savannah and the Cowgirl Ms. B

Arieahn Matamonasa Bennett

In late summer of 2010, a woman contacted me through my practice website to inquire about equine-assisted therapy (EAP) for her elderly and frail mother. This sounded like a risky prospect; however, on getting more information I understood why she wanted EAP. Her mother (Ms. B) had a horse when she was a young girl and she credited her relationship with her horse for saving her from an abusive childhood home. In her late teens and 20s, this woman had been a trick rider, yet she had not had horses in her life for decades. In her current state, Ms. B had been diagnosed with dementia and had been re-traumatized by a recent necessary medical procedure and was practically catatonic. Her daughter had a flash of inspiration that if she could somehow reconnect with a horse it might save her mother once more. I agreed and we set up a meeting at my office to get us started.

When her daughter brought her to the office she was so bent over that she was practically in a fetal position. She shook constantly, could not make eye contact. Sitting still seemed to make her even more anxious so I had her hold my hand and we walked really slowly around the office, the waiting room and the hallway. She was very unsteady on her feet and rather than asking a lot of questions, I just talked about my horses. I asked her if she wanted to see pictures of my horses at the barn and she could only nod. I handed her a photo of my therapy horse, Savannah, and told her she could keep it. She rocked back and forth and tears started streaming down her cheeks. I asked her if she wanted to meet my horse and she nodded. We set up a second session for the following week at the stable.

At our next session at the barn, she was standing much more upright. She was still very slow and unsteady on her feet. She really lit up when she saw Savannah for the first time. We kept the activities simple and she just brushed her for most of the session. Savannah, the wise therapy mare that she was, stepped ever so gingerly and carefully when around

DOI: 10.4324/9781003204534-6

Ms. B. Toward the end of the hour, Ms. B asked if I wanted her to teach me how to get Savannah to take a bow. I agreed and we set that as our plan for the next session.

As crazy as this sounds, Ms. B showed up at our next session standing practically straight, she had a cowgirl hat on, a big western belt buckle and lipstick. She was like a different person from the woman I met a few short weeks ago. Her daughter, who sometimes spoke to her like she was a child, was talking through the start of our session and Ms. B actually spoke up for the first time and said, "Shut up dearie! I'm trying to talk to Dr. Bennett." In that session, she used sugar cubes as a treat and a series of small steps to get Savannah to take a bow. As we were leaving the barn, she said "I never thought I'd ever meet a doctor like you" and I replied "I've learned a lot from you Ms. B" and she said, "Oh – I don't know about that!"

We had a few more sessions that fall until Ms. B suffered a bad fall and had to stop coming to the barn. Her daughter shared with me that after the sessions, her mother was lucid and talkative and filled with stories about her life that she had never heard before. While she would slip back into her dementia in the days following our session, her daughter said that the time after her EAP sessions were precious gifts because she got her mother "back" for those hours.

Ms. B and her daughter relocated out of state but we kept in touch and I regularly sent photos of the horses and updates from the goings on at the barn. It has now been many years but when I think of the great blessings that horses have been in my life and in the lives of my clients, this is, perhaps, my favorite story. The love of horses and the power of relationships with them that saved and sustained Ms. B during her abusive childhood also gave her life and memory back at the end of her journey. Working with Savannah and being in her presence helped Ms. B to retrieve a lost part of herself – a self who was capable, strong and determined. What was it about the horse that helped Ms. B access older parts of herself? Would this have been as effective if Ms. B did not have such a powerful history with horses? All good questions. What matters most, however, was the impact this horse had on all of our hearts.

Discussion Questions:

1   Is there evidence that connecting dementia clients with their past expertise or passions creates moments of lucidity?
2   Is there something unique about interactions with horses biologically, psychologically or spiritually that brings about change in elderly clients?

6   The Farm Was My Sun

Carol Rathmann and Sabrina Schmidt

Most children learn to love by being loved. At first, by parents and family members, and later with friends and romantic relationships. But when an infant or young child is hurt or betrayed by a parent(s) they miss that early opportunity.

At Forget Me Not Farm, we teach children to care for abused, neglected and abandoned animals. Many of the animals have stories similar to the children in our program. Our program is designed to build trusting healthy relationships, heal past traumas and learn to respect all living things.

For 30 years, thousands of at-risk children have come to Forget Me Not Farm and learned to be kind, gentle and loving. This story is about one of these children, a young girl named Sabrina.

Sabrina first came to Forget Me Not Farm as a frightened, confused and lonely child. She had been removed from an abusive family with no warning after eight years and over 23 complaints of abuse to Child Protective Services. The very next day she came to Forget Me Not Farm.

Although Sabrina was shy with the humans at the farm, she was in awe of the animals. Her intimidation by their size was quickly replaced by amazement at their gentleness. Her first love was Honey, a 33-year-old horse that had been abused for years and was sway backed and covered with scars. Her traumatic past mirrored Sabrina's. They had an immediate connection and Honey stood calmly as Sabrina gently brushed her and whispered things in her ears. It was a mutually respectful connection.

Raymond was a steer that came to Forget Me Not Farm as a baby bull calf from a dairy ranch. As a male, he was of no use to the dairy rancher and was destined for the auction yard. Fortunately, we were able to rescue him. At the farm, we bottle fed him for months and showered him with love and affection. Sabrina spent many hours laying by his side as he basked in the sun. Even when he grew to 2,000 pounds that

DOI: 10.4324/9781003204534-7

did not dampen her enthusiasm, in fact, she felt it just meant there was more of him to love.

A more playful relationship existed between Sabrina and Buddy. Buddy was the resident goat and always seemed happy when Sabrina was around. He would stand up on his hind legs and paw at his stall door until Sabrina noticed him. He loved the attention she lavished on him and would create quite a fuss when she had to leave.

What Sabrina learned at Forget Me Not Farm were lessons missed in her infancy. She learned that she was lovable. She learned to give love and to receive love. Her relationships with the animals were reciprocal – they enjoyed their time with her as much as she did with them. She even managed to care for a couple of abandoned emus that showed up in our barn one morning. While staff were hesitant to get near them, Sabrina laughed as they pecked at her head and pulled off her hair clips. We enlisted her to help us get them to the trailer when we found a new home for them. While the farm staff never got over their fear of the emus, Sabrina was fearless around them.

Sabrina never returned to her biological family. She was in the child welfare system until her 18th birthday. During her ten years in the "system" she moved several times. She lived with individual foster families, group homes and institutions. During that time, she continued to receive services at Forget Me Not Farm. We were the constant in her life. This is what Sabrina says about her time at the farm.

> The Forget Me Not Farm has impacted my life since I first set foot on the farm at eight years old. Being at the farm was the highlight of my week, time slowed down and I could just be. I was there in that moment with the animals, not worrying about other problems in my life. I had a lot of anxiety as a kid and that melted away in the moments of stroking Honey the horse's mane or playfully head butting with Buddy the goat. I still have anxiety but it is better and the farm helped me realize a therapy animal like my cat would be a helpful tool in managing it. There were so many little lessons I learned at the farm: patience, kindness, empathy, and boundaries. The farm nurtured my love and compassion for animals as a child and still continues to do so to this day. **The farm was my sun and I would orbit until my stars aligned and I could be where I was happiest.**

Sabrina visited the farm until she was 18 years old. The skills she learned from her animal interactions helped her develop healthy relationships with humans. I had the privilege to be Sabrina's mentor and her good friend. Today she is 33 years old, is an exceptional cat guardian and foster parent for young kittens. She works as a para-transit driver and has been recognized with awards for her exemplary care of her disabled passengers. When she sees a stray or abandoned animal, she does her best to bring the animal to safety for her experiences at The Forget Me Not Farm have taught her the power and value of a loving safe place.

Discussion Questions:

1   Research suggests that child abuse is known to repeat itself from generation to generation. Is it possible to prevent that repetition by providing animal assisted interventions that teach children kindness, caring and nurturing skills?

2   Children living in out-of-home placements often suffer disproportionality from attachment disorders and dysregulation. Can participation in programs promoting animal care, humane education, relationship building and prosocial behaviors help mitigate some of their undesirable behaviors?

3   Children learn empathy by observation. When a child is raised in a violent or abusive family there may not be empathic role models. Do you think it is possible for children of any age to learn and to feel empathy toward humans or animals?

7 When the Cute Factor Becomes Something More

How a Mini Donkey Taught Me the Power of the Human-Animal Bond

Christina Carr

What is context? The details that paint a picture of who we are. In a movie, it is the time period, the set design and the costumes. In social services, it's observations and assessments that inform best practices. In animal assisted interventions, we utilize social and cultural context to remove barriers and ensure that the interactions are effective and appropriate.

On a fall morning, cool and calm, while working at the barn, I helped bring in the herd of mini donkeys from the fields. Soon they were groomed and ready for a visit. The location was already chosen and assessed for safety and suitability, and the donkeys were ready for interactions. I led one of the senior herd members, Bella, into an open-space common room in a memory care facility. I saw residents sitting here and there, arriving from their respective rooms and seated throughout the room, sitting quietly in their own worlds.

Bella, a miniature donkey with boots on, and I entered first as other teams made their rounds. We were quiet and there wasn't much commotion at first. We stopped in and started walking around the room. Bella made a beeline for someone off in the corner, someone just in the corner of my eye whom I had not fully seen yet. As we approached, I saw him more clearly, in a blue polo and grey pants, Jim was easily in his 90s and was not verbal or responsive to us. Slumped in a lounge chair, Jim seemed to be elsewhere. Bella wasn't too big, and her height placed her head right at average seated lap level. She stood there, next to Jim, with her head close to his hip, no sudden movements or tension from either. She was there and he was there. I said hello and kept my eye on Bella, as my training as a handler had imbedded. And I let her do the work, the work of just being.

After about 5 minutes, something happened. A shift occurred in Jim, and something beautiful began to unfold. All I can say is that Jim's face

DOI: 10.4324/9781003204534-8

lit up as if he had just arrived in this space. His body language opened, and he moved his head toward Bella. In a smooth movement, Bella stepped up closer, and in seconds Jim's head was met with Bella's face. And for about 10 minutes they both just rested in that moment. Bella with her head angled up, her muzzle against Jim, his cheek softly resting on her short softer facial hair. In these moments, Jim's breath changed. He began breathing fuller; he was clearly in the moment, and Bella was right there with him. She exuded a calm contentment. And just like that, Jim's previously unresponsive countenance began an even more dramatic shift. He smiled, lifted his head up and, with his hand still on Bella, turned to me. He saw me, as if Bella had just introduced us. Jim told me about his family's farm. Riding horses to visit his grandparents who lived just over the holler and loving the smell of hay in the morning. Jim remembered. He was present, all while finding Bella's favorite scratch spot in her ears. I was astounded. I didn't know Jim knew I was there, I didn't know he had something to say, and the staff around me reacted in a way that let me know Jim's sudden behavior was far from a common occurrence.

The connection between Jim and Bella reminded me why I do the work I do, and why friendships, interactions and moments between humans and non-human animals are so important. Stepping into the day as a handler, I hadn't fully seen the context – we were visiting a rural senior center in an area of the south where farming and working farms were essential and still present. Where donkeys and horses lived in a different partnership with those who cared for them, and where Jim had bonded with and learned to read the needs of the animals around him, all the while, enjoying their company. Bella's context was that she has grown up around families like Jim's. She was affectionate and loved having her muzzle and ears scratched, a preference that went unnoticed by most. Most people were too shy or didn't take the time to warm up to her, to learn her favorite scratch spots. Jim and Bella connected and were able to be in the present moment with each other in a way that transcended and connected time and space. It is moments like this that make me thankful for my time with Bella and my ability to share her with others.

Discussion Questions:

1   How is context measured clinically? After reading this story, are there any questions about context or animal related interactions history that you may want to add to a biopsychosocial assessment or intake form?

2 Taking a moment to think about the mechanisms at play, what theoretical frameworks lend themselves for this type of here and now experiential therapy?
3 Cultural implications: How might context increase or decrease accessibility to animal assisted interactions?

8   Meet Roger, the Blind Sheep Helping Children Heal

Brenda Rynders

When I first moved to the West coast in 2017, one of my primary goals was to bring animal-assisted interventions into my therapeutic work. At the time, I was a newly practicing counselor with a thirst for knowledge and a vigorous passion for animal-assisted therapy. After making the leap from the Midwest to California, I immediately became involved with nonprofit sanctuaries that focused on farm animal rescue, and in 2019, I found my place at an amazing sanctuary in Sonoma called Charlie's Acres. Charlie's Acres provides a forever home to over 150 farmed animals, many of them saved from animal agriculture industries. In many ways, these animals reminded me of the clients I've worked with, showing significant symptoms of post-traumatic stress from their past experiences. I not only wanted to help these animals find inner healing, but I also desired to share their stories with individuals in the community to foster compassion and shift the ways in which these animals are viewed. Not only was I fortunate to be able to share their inspiring tales with sanctuary visitors of all ages, but I was also able to reach my therapeutic goals in 2020 with the creation of an animal-assisted therapy program at Charlie's Acres.

In this program, one of the organizations I worked with was Sonoma Mentoring Alliance, a local nonprofit that focuses on providing encouragement, support, and empowerment to at-risk youth through mentorship with positive role models. Children come to the sanctuary and engage in a variety of activities to increase their self-esteem, build confidence, and nurture their development of new skills. Throughout our visits, participants have the opportunity to interact with many sanctuary residents, such as the goofy goats and cuddly cows. However, one of the most popular animal groups amongst children is the sheep, and one sheep in particular named Roger always brought smiles to the children's faces, despite his inability to see their expressions. You see,

DOI: 10.4324/9781003204534-9

Roger came to Charlie's Acres about three years ago after suffering from severe neurological damage from a head injury, leading him to become completely blind. When Roger first arrived at the sanctuary, he was incredibly fearful of people and his new surroundings, but he soon found solace in his friendship with another sheep named Mama. Like Roger, Mama is also very special, having only three legs after she was attacked by a wild animal at her previous home. Roger and Mama have such a special bond that Mama wears a collar with a tiny silver bell so Roger can always know where his best friend is in the pasture. Although Roger cannot see Mama, he uses his powerful sense of hearing to listen for the sound of Mama's bell and he happily prances in her direction whenever he wants to be near her. Roger's story is truly inspiring, and I have shared his story many times to illustrate how inner strength, perseverance, and confidence can help anyone (people or animals) cope and even thrive, despite life's challenges. By introducing children to Roger, I have been able to teach them about the many ways in which animals are similar to us. These connections have encouraged these children to find a new appreciation for animals and nature while encouraging their own inner healing in the process.

One of Roger's biggest fans was an incredibly bright young lady "Alice". Like many children in the program, Alice came to the program from an unstable home environment and her mentor thought that the animal-assisted therapy program would be a great fit for her due to her remarkable love for art and animals. I will never forget the joy that Alice expressed the first time she laid eyes on Roger, and after hearing his story, she was instantly smitten. Alice continued to visit Roger and with each visit, I incorporated activities to allow her creativity to shine like reading to Roger or drawing colorful pictures for the animals. After one of her visits, we surprised Alice by giving her a painting that Roger himself created (using acrylic paints, a canvas print, plastic wrap, and his adorable nose) so she could always have a piece of Roger with her in her home. It's because of children like Alice that I continue to have a profound passion for animal-assisted therapy and the incredible impact it has on our hearts.

Discussion Questions:

1   After hearing Roger's story, do you believe there is a difference between the relationships we form with companion animals (household dogs, cats, small pets, etc.) and the bonds we experience with

non-companion animals (farmed animals, wildlife, captive animals in zoos, etc.)?

2 What are some additional ways children can benefit from animal-assisted interventions with non-companion animals (farmed animals, wildlife, captive animals in zoos, etc.)?

Part 2
Small Animals

9 Guinea Pigs Are Great!

Patti Anderson

Rosa

Rosa was frozen again. The second-grade classroom she sat in was warm enough but the other children were all impatiently waiting for her to continue reading the story. She struggled along, stopping and starting, clutching the book she was reading from.

Rosa was a shy second grader with thick and shiny black hair. She loved playing on the tire swing at lunch with her friends and enjoyed school, except for reading out loud in class. One day her teacher decided to partner her with a new reading assistant, with hopes that it would bolster her confidence to read out loud.

Rosa's "tutor" arrived on Friday, a furry white and gold-colored guinea pig, named "Bonita". "A 'cabayo'", exclaimed Rosa in Spanish, "We had these back home, before I moved here!"

She started speaking excitedly in Spanish to Bonita. The small animal responded by moving forward in her basket toward her. "I know what you want", mused Rosa as she leaned over and grabbed some cilantro out of a plastic bag nearby. Rosa delighted in watching Bonita "vacuum up" the leafy greens. She stroked her fur that stuck out in every direction and said to her that she certainly was a beautiful little girl.

Rosa settled down to read story after story to Bonita whom looked at the pictures in the book and seemed to follow along. The two of them enjoyed reading together throughout the several weeks of their tutoring sessions. When they finished, Rosa returned to her classroom for reading time and was asked to introduce her new friend, Bonita, to the other children.

Rosa proceeded to show her classmates how to pet a "cabayo". They delighted in giving her a treat too. Rosa had selected Bonita's favorite guinea pig story to read out loud to the class. Her teacher smiled knowingly, as Rosa read the story skillfully out loud and with confidence.

DOI: 10.4324/9781003204534-11

The time came when Rosa had to say goodbye to her tiny mentor. With pride, she used a bookmark with Bonita's photo on it every time she read, to remind her of her favorite reading buddy.

Abdi

Abdi was disengaged from the other teens in the day treatment center he attended. He wanted to be accepted by the other students but the staff said he had difficulty in "self-regulating". Abdi knew that just meant he fidgeted a lot and was easily distracted.

The social workers had tried to teach Abdi some new strategies for calming his mind and body. He had tried, but nothing seemed to take hold. The group sessions were the most difficult for Abdi as he just couldn't sit still and would blurt out something when another teen was talking.

The treatment center had a facility dog, "Tucker", a friendly golden retriever that came several times a week. When Tucker was in group sessions, Abdi was quieter. However, that was due to him feeling intimidated by dogs, as they were never a part of the culture he had grown up in.

One day, there was an announcement to the students that there would be an AAT (Animal Assisted Therapy) program at the center, incorporating several species, starting with guinea pigs!

When the students arrived for their first AAT session, they gathered around a long desk where a yoga mat had been placed. Surrounding the length of the mat was a short safety fence.

The students were instructed that they would individually try to lead their guinea pig partner in a "trust walk" across the yoga mat, to the small blue plastic house at the end of it. They used slivers of carrots to entice them. If the student moved too quickly, talked loudly or wasn't focused, the guinea pig would decide to run back into the safety of their "house".

Abdi was the last student to have a turn. He had little interest in this activity, until he overheard some students whispering, saying he wouldn't be able to do it at all. Feeling defensive and challenged, he stepped up to the mat.

Hermione (named after one of the Harry Potter characters) wouldn't budge out of her "hidey hole" for Abdi. He remembered that guinea pigs responded better to someone who was calm, so decided to try some strategies he had learned. With deep concentration, he focused his efforts, and they paid off! Hermione trusted him to lead her to the end of the mat.

Abdi was ecstatic! He had shown the other students that he could do this. It was one of the few times he had been successful. Abdi finally felt what it was like to be able to relax his mind and body, even if it was just for a few minutes.

It reminded him of when he was younger and learned how to ride his bike. When the training wheels were removed, everything just "clicked" as he felt in his body what it was like to balance. He was able to ride a bicycle from that moment on.

Hermione had been the bridge needed to help Abdi experience what it felt like to be able to calm himself during the "Trust Walk" session. That feeling carried over to the group session later in the day. He applied what he had learned, enjoying positive feedback from the other students after the session. Like her namesake, Hermione shared a little magic with Abdi that day.

Discussion Questions:

1   How can the name of an animal, enhance and support the AAI experience?

2   What does an AAI practitioner need to know regarding the cultural differences of the people they are working with? List some reputable resources for current information regarding this subject.

3   What information should be included in the informed consent document the participant might receive regarding an AAI program?

10 The Bunnies Are In

Jennifer A. Coleman

I was in graduate school, working toward my doctorate in counseling psychology, specializing in human-animal interactions. It had been an emotionally difficult year and I knew having some companionship would improve my mood and reduce my feelings of isolation. If my apartment and lifestyle had afforded me such, I would likely have gotten a dog. Instead, one winter day I brought home a young rabbit, weighing less than a pound. Zeus is a caramel-colored Lop with streaks and spots of gray mixed in. His fur is as soft as velvet and if you met him, he might bump you with his nose as a sign of affection. He will eat out of your hand, and bananas and dried papaya are his favorite treats. In my graduate school apartment, he had access to free roam, doing zoomies up and down the carpeted hallway. On weekends, I often took him outside on a leash to run about. As an adult Lop, both of his ears flop straight down, but as a kitten, he had helicopter ears (his left stood straight up; his right flopped straight down). He is bold and unphased, even when meeting dogs bigger than him. He is an incredibly social rabbit and as a result, he has met many kittens and dogs I have fostered.

At school, in addition to courses and clinical work, I worked as an assistant clinical director at the University's community outpatient clinic. Two graduate students and I worked in a windowless brick room, conducting pre-intake phone calls with potential clients and assisting clinical staff who were mostly other graduate students or clinical trainees. Our role as assistant clinical directors varied, but it often involved a lot of logistics. We would check in and out assessment material to trainees or remind them that they needed to finalize clinical documents in their clients' electronic health records. Interactions were typically brief and to the point.

One year while I worked at the clinic, I was also a research assistant on a study that examined the benefits of therapy dogs for children with autism. We coded video interactions of the children and these dogs.

DOI: 10.4324/9781003204534-12

I loved the idea of having a therapy dog for sessions with clients or even a facility dog to improve the mood among staff. I do not recall how the idea came about, but at some point, I proposed to the clinic director the idea of bringing Zeus into the clinic.

The clinic director was very supportive of this idea and we eventually got the right people to sign off. I started to bring Zeus to work with me a few days a week. Soon, word spread to the staff and clinical trainees. The dynamic in the office changed. Clinicians and staff started to knock on our office door just to ask "is Zeus in?" before proceeding to sit on the ground to pet or feed Zeus. Eventually, I got Zeus a mate, a black rabbit I rescued from the local SPCA, whom I named Kizmet. Our office now had a pair of bunny visitors. A friend of mine created a sign for the outside of our office doors that mimicked the Peanut's cartoon: "Psychiatric Help 5¢. The doctor is in." Our sign read, "Psychiatric Help 5¢. The bunnies are in."

It amazed me how the simple act of bringing a bunny to work had such a profound effect on the office dynamics. Staff started coming into our office because they were having a bad day and knew petting Zeus would lift their spirits. Clinical trainees, after a challenging session with a client, would interact with Zeus and share their struggles or consult on cases with us. Perhaps unsurprisingly, staff often voiced disappointment if they came to work and Zeus was at home. Zeus not only made my life and home less lonely, he helped connect my colleagues in a unique way. He was truly a gift to all who met him and he continues to be a gift to me.

> Always nice to have a bunny break.
> Peer Assistant Director & Clinical Trainee

> I loved having our rabbit guests at our training clinic! It was great to have them there for a work break and some stress relief. It was also special to see how everyone- whether it was trainees, staff, faculty- took the time to say hello and focus on the animals instead of work for a moment. They were great to have around!
> Peer Assistant Director & Clinical Trainee

> Time after time, I found stressed students on the floor of your office, feeding and petting them. The calming effect they had on students was readily apparent. In fact, students and staff were routinely disappointed when they came to the clinic on a day there were no bunny therapists in the office!
> Clinic Director

Discussion Questions:

1   What do you see as some pros and cons for staff to having an animal in an office setting?
2   What do you see as some pros and cons for an animal that is brought into an office setting?
3   What are some differences between Zeus and a therapy animal?

11 Wait – My Therapy Animal Is a … Rat?

Angela K. Fournier

This is a story about Hillary and Honey, my pet rats and colleagues, who surprised everyone with their warm personalities and sweet spirits. Hillary and Honey lived with my family and frequently joined me at work in the Department of Psychology at Bemidji State University.

My students and I conduct research on animal-assisted interventions. In the spring of 2015, we were curious about whether visiting with animals benefited college students, and if so, how? We conducted a study where student volunteers spent time in the laboratory with an animal and then completed questionnaires. We were interested in people's reactions to different species, so our research partners included Hillary and Honey, as well as several dogs and cats. When recruiting participants, students were told they could possibly spend time with one of these animals. Once they were in the laboratory, they were told which animal was present that day. They were free to discontinue if the animal was a species they were allergic to, afraid of, or just uncomfortable with.

People had mixed reactions when told they would be interacting with rats – from excitement to disgust. *"Oh cute!"* and *"Oh gross!"* were the two most common responses. Quite a few students had signed up hoping they would spend time with a dog; they were surprised and a bit disappointed to find out it was a rat day in the lab. However, no one withdrew from the study or even requested a different animal.

For the study, Hillary and Honey were in a room that contained rat treats, toys, and a brush. Students rated their mood, spent 5–10 minutes of unstructured time with the rats, and then rated their mood again. Students reported feeling happier and more relaxed after engaging with an animal – any animal – dog, cat, or rat. Our next question was how? What was it about spending time with animals that made them feel good? For the rats, it seems related to their physical appearance and

DOI: 10.4324/9781003204534-13

behavior. Students commented about how soft their fur was, how sweet their eyes looked, and that in general, they were "cute." They enjoyed watching them, feeding them treats, and holding and petting them.

The rats were not trained to perform any particular behaviors; they just needed to be themselves and students enjoyed watching their natural behavior. Rats are inherently good at foraging for food and hiding it, and Hillary and Honey were no exception. They had a habit of hiding treats within their enclosure, burying them under the bedding. They also hid food outside of their enclosure, creating stockpiles in corners and under furniture within the observation room. Students enjoyed watching Hillary and Honey store food, expressing surprise at their intelligence and pleasure in witnessing their creativity.

Sometimes what was enjoyable was the dynamic interaction *between* Hillary and Honey. Students thought it was "adorable" when they groomed each other or slept next to one another. They found humor when they antagonized each other. Both rats would take treats from an individual's hand and then hide them. Hillary had a habit of taking Honey's treats out of her hiding spot and moving them into her own. Several students observed this and got great enjoyment from it. Even students who maintained negative associations with rats found some enjoyment from the experience. One student wrote, "*I couldn't touch them because they gross me out. But I enjoyed watching them interact with each other.*"

For many students, the experience changed the way they thought about rats. One student said, "*Going in I thought all rats would be gross and grey. But the rats were smaller than expected, very soft, kind of cute and very easy to be around.*" Another student said, "*I learned that not all rats are gross. They were very soft, had cool tails, and seemed friendly.*" As you can see, the perception of rats as "*gross*" was a theme, as was the shift toward acknowledging some redeeming qualities.

As a researcher, the experience of working with Hillary and Honey helped me understand that each species can assist humans in their own way. Hillary and Honey brought happiness and joy to students, just as much as the other animals did. But the way in which they elicited these emotions may be unique to rats and perhaps other pocket pets (e.g., hamsters, mice). Students practiced quiet observation and slow, gentle movements. They experienced novelty and surprise. Hillary and Honey helped everyone feel a little better for a little while, and for some students facilitated a shift in their thinking from negative assumptions and disgust to appreciation. By just being themselves, Hillary and Honey brought students the gifts of a brighter day and a broader perspective.

Discussion Questions:

1 Can any species animal serve as therapy animal? Why or why not?
2 How might animal-assisted therapy be different when the therapy animal is a rat versus a dog?
3 Some of the students in this story had preconceived ideas about rats. Discuss factors that influence client responses to different therapy animals.

12 A Crystallized Connection

Julie Ann Nettifee

On a snow-covered pathway lined with bunny paws, Christmas 2010 became the year that a pair of Dutch Belgian bunnies joined our home, bunnies discarded because they did not have the qualities the breeder desired. What the breeder did not know at the time was that these two were meant for a show he could not have imagined. The "show" they were destined for was much, much greater. They were born with gifts that were not evident to the hands that bred them. Yet as they started their lives with a young boy with sensory processing needs, their greater purpose began to unfold. Just as the unwrapping of a holiday gift, both rabbits began to blossom with personality, sensitivity, compassion, and love. Bunnies, in a spirit realm, can represent a positive sign for a new beginning and the opportunity to start anew. This one child had already started his journey years before, facing hearing loss, sensory processing, and other challenges. Yet almost instinctively, even though his sensory processing often was demonstrated by firm pressure, he seemed to sense that the bunnies were creatures that needed a very gentle touch and a quiet presence.

The pair of bunnies, named Crystal and Boulder, after the stones that this young boy would line every pocket with, both began to shine in their new environment. Their new assignment not only included this young boy, Jordan, but also other young children on the sensory processing spectrum as well as seniors in assisted therapy, as these two groups met and interacted with one another. Connected by their own gifts, and now with therapy bunnies, they joined in conversation, connection, and love. Boulder, as his name implied, was a bit more "solid" and although he enjoyed petting, brushing, and attention, he was a bit more stoic in his approach. Crystal, named after a sparkling gem, had one crystal blue eye and one brown eye. Jordan would often say that her blue eye "sparkled like a diamond". As the caregiver for both my son and the bunnies, I would watch in amazement as their ability to connect helped him flourish in his sensory and speech therapy.

DOI: 10.4324/9781003204534-14

Part of the program for Jordan and the bunnies was therapy involving a small group of neurotypical and neurodiverse children and local nursing home residents. All welcomed Crystal and Boulder who provided opportunities to learn about the human-animal bond. When each new week would come, Jordan arranged their travel kennels, excitedly loaded into the waiting Toyota, and traveled to local visit sites. On one particular day, Jordan was holding Crystal while a resident named Lorraine asked to see her more closely. The staff watched in amazement, as Lorraine had shared very little with them since entering the dementia unit months prior. Jordan with his angelic smile gently set Crystal down on Lorraine's lap. The story began, with Lorraine going back to a childhood memory, when she, too, had a Dutch Belgian bunny. She spoke of him fondly and recalled how peaceful she felt when she held it. The soft, velvet fur offered a sensory experience that took her down a memory lane traveled many years ago relived in an instant with the stroke of this bunny. Crystal was a "master" at her job. With her blue eye, the one that sparkled like a clear quartz, she could help even the most agitated child or senior. Like the crystal stone with healing properties, this liver and white Dutch bunny had her own powers.

Jordan is now a young man and his sensitivity to life, love, and connection is undeniable. One powerful story, shared by Jordan, was the day he was riding in the Toyota, and recalled how another little boy, with challenges similar to the ones that he has faced, shared with him that the bunnies helped him to connect more with those around him – just by their peaceful presence. The stories Jordan shares of his time doing therapeutic outreach are remarkable to all who know him. The best-kept secret is that while Jordan was providing outreach and therapy to others through his connection with his bunnies, the gifts he was sharing allowed for his own growth.

At times in our lives, the crystals we are drawn to are the crystals that we need for healing. In this case, the Crystal had four paws, an amazing heart, and offered healing for all who crossed her path.

Discussion Questions:

1 In what ways could a species such as the rabbit in this story be incorporated into therapeutic techniques?
2 How does sensory processing disorder manifest in individuals?
3 What types of therapeutic interventions could benefit from the model described in the "crystallized" connection?

13 Sullivan Anne

From Abandoned Rabbit to Beloved Campus Pet Therapy Animal

Clarissa M. Palmer

I have always known how much companion animals can affect human development. After all, I have been around companion animals since I was born and have seen the direct impact that animals have on people. In my professional role, I am a university professor of education, but I also coordinate the pet therapy program on our campus. This program brings therapy animal teams on campus for special events, weekly visits to specific buildings, class presentations, and individual sessions. Most often, the therapy animals I work with are dogs. However, I have also worked with rats, horses, cows, donkeys, and goats. This is the story of Sullivan Anne, a rabbit who helps college students, staff, and faculty with stress and anxiety.

Sullivan is a rabbit who was rescued from a field down the street from our home. Neighbors watched, from a distance, as two kids left a blue blanket in the field. The neighbors drove to the location noticing there was something moving in the cloth. As they moved closer, it became clear that the "something" was a domestic rabbit! They were able to scoop her up and take her home. Despite posting notices and calling veterinarians to see if anyone reported a lost rabbit, no one stepped forward to claim her. We saw these postings and knew – we brought Sullivan home and she has been part of our family since 2018.

Sullivan took a while to warm up to her humans but very quickly warmed up to the other critters in the house, especially our tuxedo cat William. Her fixation on him allowed us to get closer to her and, eventually, pick her up and allow her to sit in our laps. As she grew accustomed to being held and petted, I could see her potential as a therapy animal. Her temperament was amazing! She was very calm while being pet and held; she did not negatively or overly react to loud noises; and she was housetrained.

DOI: 10.4324/9781003204534-15

Sullivan and I embarked on formal training to become a therapy team. This training was successful. Sullivan appeared to enjoy rides in the car and thrived in the classroom environment. In one class session, although several students were very excited to hold Sullivan, she decided one particular student needed her attention. This is one of Sullivan's great skills – she seems to know who needs time with her. It is almost as if she can sense who is feeling stressed. Sullivan fell asleep in "Mandy's" lap and basically refused to move when I tried to pick her up. Sullivan shifted more deeply into the students' lap and burrowed her head into the student's sweatshirt. I let Sullivan stay in this student's lap for the rest of the class period and used the opportunity to talk about how animals are sometimes able to detect people's emotions.

After class ended, with Sullivan still on her lap, Mandy and I made a plan for additional individual time with Sullivan in my office. Over the course of the fall semester, Mandy visited Sullivan weekly. These visits consisted of Mandy holding and petting Sullivan, researching rabbit behavior, and chatting with me about what was going on in her personal and academic life.

Mandy had a high degree of anxiety over schoolwork and life after graduation. She shared her fears of the unknown upon graduation: not finding a job in her field (or a job at all), feeling like she should move out of her family home, and how to navigate the major life transitions that come after school. During her visits with Sullivan, we talked about career paths and possible opportunities for employment or graduate schools. We were often joined by other faculty members would stop in to share their career journeys – and pet Sullivan.

Throughout the semester, it was clear Mandy's self-assurance grew; these "Sullivan sessions" had a positive impact across many aspects of her life. Her grades improved, her procrastination reduced, and she started to develop a plan for her life after graduation. As an extra bonus, she decided to focus her final senior art project on Sullivan.

The fall semester ended and Mandy asked if she could visit with Sullivan one last time before moving to New York City for her new job. During this visit, she brought Sullivan a bunch of carrots and two handmade ornaments. Over a year later, the ornaments still hang in my office.

Discussion Questions:

1   What relationships can you identify in this chapter? Describe the importance of the bidirectional relationships presented in this chapter.

2   What are specific developmental tasks that Sullivan and pet therapy teams can assist college-age students with throughout their college careers?

3   In what other ways might pet therapy be useful on college campuses?

14 Can I Take *Chophie* Home?

The Simple Joys of Having Animal Co-Therapists

Georgitta Valiyamattam

In the early summer of 2018, I had finished collecting data for a part of my doctoral dissertation, working with special education schools. I then signed up to conduct a few additional animal-assisted activity sessions for interested kids who had been excluded initially due to research protocols. And this is where I met "Sanjay" – a nine-year-old, largely non-verbal, autistic boy. He also had partial cataracts in both eyes – the reason why he wasn't a part of our eye-tracking research.

Both Sanjay's parents and special educators informed us that he was scared of animals in general. It seemed to make sense. He would peek into the room while we set up animal-assisted activity sessions for other kids, squeal and run away. This peek-a-boo continued for a while and then slowly, a few days into the sessions, we found Sanjay waiting by the door for longer, watching other kids interact with the guinea pigs. However, if we invited him in, he would run off. We just decided to let it be.

As we packed up one evening about two weeks later, Sanjay was still at the door. He had ambled in a few minutes before from his speech therapy classes. His expressive vocabulary comprised less than fifty words. After the other kids left, Sanjay came in hesitantly and sat on the floor. We were rather surprised as he tried to touch the guinea pig through the grid of the carrier crate. We asked him if he wanted a better look. He nodded. I took Sophie out and placed her on my lap. She was the oldest (and the wisest as we used to call her!) of our four guinea pig co-therapists. Sanjay slowly crept a bit closer and began stroking her forehead with his finger. We asked him if he wanted to groom her. He tried but had difficulty gripping the comb. Feeding Sophie was easier for him and he squealed in delight as she ate the cucumber slices that he held out. Our impromptu session with Sanjay that day lasted nearly thirty minutes.

DOI: 10.4324/9781003204534-16

A new routine started that day. Sanjay would wait patiently, peeking in, waiting for the other kids to leave. And when he came in, the guinea pigs, especially Sophie, became the center of his world. He tried his hand at the different combs we had in our kit and would make an effort to grip the comb tight. He quickly learned how to use his palms to caress Sophie. One day when Sophie showed little interest in eating the usual carrots and cucumber slices, he became very disappointed. Using words and gestures, we asked him to try something different perhaps bell pepper pieces. It took some time for him to grasp the idea, but when he did and Sophie ate them, Sanjay was ecstatic. The next day, he tried to share food from his own lunchbox and that became an opportunity for another lesson on what guinea pigs could or couldn't eat. He seemed to grasp this new lesson as well. Eventually, Sanjay also became accommodating of a younger kid who joined the impromptu sessions. A couple instances from our work with Sanjay were very special. For instance, several times we found him tilting his head and squinting just to get a better look at Sophie's face and then he would try to gently kiss her ears. We were a bit cautious as he came closer to Sophie and wondered if he was trying to sniff-a behavior seen in autism. But we soon realized that it was an affectionate kiss. He would also give flying kisses and enact Sophie returning them. We were told that such displays of emotions were otherwise rare for him. Although he liked all the guinea pigs, his favorite was *"Chophie"* – how he pronounced Sophie's name. Adding her name to his small list of spoken words was a remarkable display of his efforts to communicate verbally and delighted the staff. In fact, all our team members were either *Chophie* (if part of therapy) or not. Despite having heard similar stories before, it felt incredible how our complex social identities were now linked to a single amazing animal co-therapist.

After our last regular session at the school, we were having an informal chat with the staff. Sanjay was instructed to pack his bag as school was closing. We had been preparing Sanjay, telling him how Sophie would only be visiting occasionally after a certain date. He seemed to understand. As we chatted, Sanjay came in again, this time with his school bag emptied out. He said *Chophie*, pointing at her and then inside his empty bag. He wanted to take her home. With the best of our preparation for possible instances as these, we fumbled as we explained how Sophie had to visit other kids and though not as often as now, we promised we would bring her to visit him. He nodded squatting by the carrier cage, reaching out to Sophie. We fell silent, all of us filled with emotion, struck by how extraordinary it was to be part of that simple moment. We reflected on all that we had witnessed over the past weeks and vowed (and succeeded) in keeping our promise – it was not the last time that Sanjay was able to visit with *Chophie*.

Discussion Questions:

1   Why do you think autistic children demonstrate strong connections with animals despite general social functioning deficits?
2   How can we best prepare children for transitions, such as the close of animal-assisted intervention sessions or a new therapy animal?

15 The Rabbit Who Knew No Rules

Patti Anderson

The little girl had been in the hospital for many weeks. One afternoon, she suddenly burst into tears, crying uncontrollably, when her parents wanted to leave her room to go and speak with the doctor.

"Jada, honey, we will be in that little conference room down the hall and be back really soon." said her mother, looking exhausted.

"I don't care!" Jada yelled back, rubbing her bald head, "I want you to stay!"

Just then, a pink baby stroller rolled into the room with two large white, fuzzy ears sticking up out of the top. Everyone stopped talking and stared at the hospital volunteer pushing it.

"Hi," she greeted, "I'm Barb and this is Esther. Would you like a visit today?" she asked while directing her question to the young patient in the bed.

"What's an Esther?" questioned Jada, sniffing a little bit and wiping the tears off her face with a tissue. "She's a therapy bunny that loves being pet," answered Barb. "Would you like to pet her?" Jada slowly nodded her head up and down, looking back at her parents, a bit warily.

"Jada, your Dad and I will be right down the hall while you visit with the rabbit, ok?" said her mother.

"Okay" mumbled Jada as a large white ball of fuzz was lifted out of the pet stroller and onto her bed. Jada pushed her IV stand over to the side to make more room for Esther. She noticed that the rabbit's legs were splayed out and that she laid flat on her stomach instead of resting on her haunches. "What's wrong with her?" Jada asked quietly, as Esther nudged her to be pet.

Before responding, Barb showed Jada how to stroke Esther's long ears, which was one of her favorite spots to be pet.

Esther was born with something called "Swimmer's Syndrome" where she has to move by pulling herself forward on her tummy.

DOI: 10.4324/9781003204534-17

Esther hasn't known anything different and doesn't care how she looks or moves as that is just how she is.

"Oh." responded Jada, furrowing her brows, "sort of like how I look really different with no hair?" Barb continued, "Esther is still who she is inside, no matter how she looks on the outside and right now she is loving having you pet her!" The large brown eyes of the rabbit (that had been posted on Criag's List as snake food) met the eyes of the little girl in the Sesame Street pajamas. As the two new friends connected, a slow, heartfelt smile traveled across Jada's face.

She continued to whisper quietly to Esther, while continuing to pet her. Jada's words were meant only for the bunny beside her on the bed. After a while, Jada rested her bald head near Esther's fluffy body feeling warm and safe. She snuggled in even more, soon falling sound asleep.

As Jada's parents returned to their daughter's room, Barb and Esther started to leave quietly, not wanting to wake up the little girl. Jada's mother mouthed "thank you" to Barb as she wheeled past her, tearing up a bit as they left the room.

Sometimes it is difficult to know if a therapy animal makes a difference in someone's life, as you might only see that person once for a brief interaction and not know if they had any impact. It is unusual to cross paths with family member later on, especially after a hospital visit, so Barb was amazed when that actually happened.

Two years after the visit with Jada, Barb was volunteering at a school for disabled children with about fifteen other rabbit handlers. "Rabbit Day" was an annual event at this school, one which the students always looked forward to. One of the kindergarten teachers approached the group wringing her hands and tentatively asked if anyone knew a rabbit named Esther. Barb stepped forward and introduced herself, and, smiling widely, said "Esther was my sweet girl!"

The teacher had chalk dust on her hands that made a slight dust cloud in the air when she clapped them together, exclaiming "I am so excited you are here and that we have connected. I want to thank you for all that you have done!"

"Let me explain," she continued.

Esther visited my niece at the hospital several years ago when Jada was really sick and not doing well. All Jada has talked about off and on since then is about the fluffy white bunny who was her friend during that tough time. Jada is now disease-free and doing well, but remembers the day Esther visited, giving her the gift of peace and hope, something she will always remember.

Esther's calm, loving presence made a positive impact on many children's lives over the years. She had an indomitable spirit and an easygoing personality that enjoyed the attention from everyone she met. Barb appreciated the positive comments from those they visited, as many shared that Esther opened their eyes to possibilities that they thought they couldn't undertake. They would comment that, if this sweet rabbit could persevere in life, then so could they.

Barb said that Esther will be remembered as the bunny that knew no rules, living her life to the fullest.

Discussion Questions:

1   List the pros and cons of partnering in AAI with a physically disabled animal? Discuss this topic from the viewpoint of the humans involved and also from the animal's perspective.

2   What are some of the health (disease transmissions) and physical safety steps (to prevent bites/scratches) a responsible therapy animal handler should take to protect the people they interact with on a visit? Please include how they should also protect their animal.

16 Who *Are* You?

Niki Vettel

"What's that – a rat?"

I was sitting in the group room on the eighth floor in the locked forensic psychiatric facility in downtown Boston. The "rat" in question was Ralphie, my Pet Partners® registered pet therapy guinea pig. Ralphie, an Abyssinian breed, was a redhead with a sworl of cowlicks who generally elicited spontaneous outbursts of "I LOVE him!" from those who met him.

I looked at the stocky young man who had entered the room. He sported a pair of "ninja" wrap-around sunglasses that gave him a menacing look. The Solomon Carter Fuller Health Center's forensic locked units were on floors 4, 5, and 8, and I had learned that the eighth floor generally housed the most difficult, and potentially violent, patients.

Smiling, I looked down at Ralphie, who was sitting in his visiting cozy, and replied, "No, he's not a rat. He's a guinea pig." "Huh," the visitor said. "Sure looks like a rat." Checking out this guy, I made a quick calculation: despite the glasses, he had a sense of humor. "He's much cuter than a rat," I offered. "Well, still looks like a rat," he said. Then a pause. "Can I pet the rat?"

The other person in the group room was my facilitator, who always accompanied me in my visits, a security measure that our local Pet Partners® group, Paws for People, and the facility, insisted upon. My facilitator, a therapist himself, kept a low profile, allowing me and Ralphie to run the groups and direct the conversations.

The young man, "Scott," quickly became one of Ralphie's most ardent fans. He attended every visit we made and was a quick study in learning the appropriate way to feed, pet, and hold his cozy, and Ralphie, for his part, demonstrated complete trust in Scott.

Ralphie made his visits sitting in a "cozy" and was allowed to sit on a patient's lap if I felt a high level of comfort with that individual. In short order, Scott and Ralphie always shared lap time, and Ralphie

DOI: 10.4324/9781003204534-18

happily accepted all his favorite veggies and special treats directly from Scott's hand, would nap while Scott was brushing him, and stretch out in the gesture that said "I feel safe with you." They were a bonded pair.

One day, I chatted with a senior nurse on the unit. "You should be very careful with Scott," she cautioned me. "He's got a history of violence." I assured her that Scott had shown nothing but affection and care for Ralphie. She looked skeptical. A few weeks later, she and I caught up again. "It's amazing," she said to me. "Scott is a different person after these visits with you and your animal."

One day at the end of our visit, Scott asked if he could kiss Ralphie good-night. It was a surprising show of tenderness from this big man who presented tough and gruff. Of course, it was alright. So Scott would gently kiss Ralphie on the top of his head; he said he hated to see him go.

Our bi-monthly visits were going well and we generally made casual observations about Ralphie's diet and amusing antics; sometimes, I simply observed Scott and the other patients in the group interacting with each other and Ralphie. But one day Scott's talk turned personal.

He told me that he had called his parents, and that they had refused to speak with him. "Who *does* that?" he asked me. He was clearly in emotional pain. It was not a rhetorical question, and I did not have an answer. My role at the facility was not intended to be individually clinical in nature; we visited to help patients relax, feel "normal" and have a tactile experience with Ralphie since all the units were no-touch. Being able to hold and pet this two-pound ball of fur was a deeply moving experience for many of the group members. But Scott posed that question, with a piercing sense of urgency. I felt honored he had opened up to me but inadequate in my ability to respond. I duly reported the exchange to my facilitator and he was surprised. Scott was not a guy who talked about his feelings. Ever.

Then, Scott missed several of our visits. He had physically lashed out at another patient and his pet visit privilege had been suspended. When he rejoined us, we didn't mention his absence. He was just glad to see Ralphie again, and vice versa.

Scott spent his time brushing Ralphie, feeding him his favorite treats, and passing the half-hour with pleasant conversation. He liked to talk directly to Ralphie, but now he did something quite different. Sensing it was soon time to leave, he gently held Ralphie up to his face; Ralphie and he locked eyes for several moments. Then Scott said directly to Ralphie, "Who *ARE* you?" Ralphie held his gaze. He carefully lowered Ralphie back onto his lap, kissed the top of his head, and we said good-bye.

I never saw Scott again. And I will never forget that final exchange. *"Who are you?"* is one of the most profound questions we can ask of another, and of ourselves. It can take years of therapy to arrive at that moment of inquiry, or, for some people, several months in the company of a small, redheaded guinea pig.

Discussion Questions:

1   Can you imagine some of the reasons that Scott bonded so closely with Ralphie?
2   What do you feel Scott meant by the question "Who are you?"

Part 3

Crisis

17 Boston in Coal City

Julie Bereckis

Boston is a Chow-Shiba Inu mix pup weighing in at about 42 lbs. She owns me but belongs to the world. She loves being with people and has a sixth sense; she just seems to know when someone needs comfort or just a tail wag or a kiss.

On Monday June 22, 2015, a tornado touched down in Coal City, Illinois. Coal City is a small town southeast of Chicago, next to Kankakee. The tornado was classified as an EF3 (on a scale from EF0 to EF5) with winds between 135 and 165 mph. Thankfully no one was seriously injured, and no lives were lost. We even learned later that no pets were lost. The Red Cross and Federal Emergency Management Agency (FEMA) quickly went to work setting up a Multi-Agency Resource Center (MARC) to help the affected families. HOPE AACR (Animal-Assisted Crisis Response) teams were invited to join in the effort. Hope AACR is an organization that oversees the mobilization of volunteer teams in response to major catastrophes. It is amazing to be on these calls and see how quickly and efficiently these agencies bring everything together.

A MARC was set up to take place over the upcoming weekend. I volunteered to go, accompanied by Boston. We arrived on Sunday not knowing what to expect as this was our first crisis MARC experience. We took a short walk outside and I prepared myself mentally for what may lie ahead. We were there about an hour when one of the volunteers approached and said she needed our help. She led Boston and I to a mother waiting in the intake line with her son behind her, hiding in the corner and hugging the wall. The volunteer introduced me to mom. I sat down with mom and she explained that her son, Timmy, had not spoken since the tornado happened. I listened, and then sat down on the floor with Boston and introduced both of us to Timmy. As if on a cue, Boston wagged her tail and looked eagerly at Timmy. At first, Timmy did not respond. So I just started talking to Timmy about Boston. As time went

DOI: 10.4324/9781003204534-20

on, Timmy slowly started to come out of the corner. I asked him if he wanted to pet Boston and feel how soft she was. He nodded yes, and as if Boston understood, she took two steps toward him and stood expectantly next to him. I asked him if he had any questions about her. At first, he said no but then as he continued to pet her, he quietly asked her age. I said she was nine and he said that was his age too. I asked him his name to which he softly replied "Timmy".

It was at this time that we moved into a private room. Boston and I sat on the floor in the middle of the room while mom sat in the corner speaking with a counselor. Timmy came and sat with us on the floor. At first, he did not want to talk so we just sat there and petted Boston. After a short time, he started talking and asking questions. I explained what a great listener Boston was. I told him he could tell Boston anything he wanted and she would never tell anyone else. He started telling Boston about the storm and how he felt. At some point, he noticed carpet squares in the corner and asked if he could get one for Boston to lay on. I said yes. He proceeded to grab a few and set them on the floor and then proceeded to lay down next to Boston. After a short while, he stood up and went to find a book. Quickly returning, he settled in next to Boston and started to read. At one point, I glanced over at mom and saw she had tears in her eyes as she nodded her approval. Eventually, Timmy told us he had a dog of his own and started telling us stories about "Buddy". Before I knew it, we had spent an hour in the room. As we transitioned back into the main area, Timmy gave Boston a hug goodbye and ran off to find his friends. It was at this point that Timmy's mom came up and thanked us; clearly relieved to see the positive change in Timmy.

Driving home, I reflected on the experience and my heart filled with happiness, knowing that Boston and I had succeeded in making one little boy's world a little brighter.

Discussion Questions:

1   Any event can affect people in various ways, the degree of post-traumatic stress disorder (PTSD) that someone feels is unique to each person. Do you agree?

2   How a person responds and copes has to do with their resiliency. Do you feel this can be taught or is it shaped through life experiences?

18 HOPE AACR Responds to Devastating Mudslide

Bette Caldwell

Imagine this scenario: your family lives in a beautiful home in Montecito, in the hills north of Santa Barbara, California. In the fall of 2017, a horrendous wildfire destroyed more than 297 acres in the area. Fortunately, firefighters were able to save Montecito, although the nearby hills were denuded and left barren.

Fast forward a few months to early January 2018. A severe rain storm moved in and residents were warned that they needed to evacuate, but few did. Then, in the middle of the night, the storm became more intense and the area was flooded, creating horrendous mudslides. Trees, large boulders, and other debris washed down from the surrounding hills, gaining strength as the storm swept through the town. Several officials described the scene as "a war zone" and "Armageddon." We learned that one family had been severely affected: the father was killed, the mother hospitalized, the 14-year-old daughter trapped in the mud seriously injured, and the 11-year-old brother missing. His body was never found.

HOPE AACR (Animal-Assisted Crisis Response) was asked to respond to this crisis. As a Team Leader, I worked closely with 6 HOPE members and their dogs. The Earl Warren Showgrounds in Santa Barbara served as the base camp for approximately 2,400 first responders, including Office of Emergency Services, Cal Fire, medical personnel, law enforcement, Conservation Corps, Urban Search and Rescue, cooks, veterinarians, military personnel, and Peer Support Team members.

Our arrival with the dogs was greeted with enthusiasm as the handlers mingled with the first responders and shared their dogs' "trading cards." We heard stories about their dogs at home and saw photos. That evening, the HOPE members attended the community vigil at the Santa Barbara Courthouse – a very moving experience. Numerous adults and children came and interacted with the dogs. A woman with two girls

DOI: 10.4324/9781003204534-21

(10 or 11 years old) approached two of the dogs and said, "These are crisis response dogs; they comfort people; you should pet them." The girls were happy to comply and began petting the two retrievers. Soon the girls were lying on the grass, totally engaged in petting and talking to the dogs.

The following day, 2 HOPE members worked with a *Federal Emergency Management Agency (FEMA)* member who was quite moved when he saw the golden retrievers. He shared that he had found a deceased golden retriever stuck up a tree the previous day. He said that it was a very emotional recovery for him ...that recovering deceased pets was as difficult for them as finding deceased people. He said that all first responders removed bodies with great respect and honor. He was upset that the dog he found wasn't wearing a collar because he wanted to give the dog's family closure.

We had many good conversations with the first responders. They were so appreciative and thankful for the opportunity to interact with the HOPE teams. Oftentimes, they shared stories and photos of their own dogs at home. It was great to see frowns turn to smiles. One HOPE member shared her interaction with a first responder.

> I heard a conversation among some firefighters and one said he was disappointed that he couldn't pet the search and rescue dogs. I encouraged him to pet my black lab and he was thrilled. He enjoyed the attention and wildly wagged his tail. When I handed him the dog's trading card, he was upset that it was not "pawtographed." (when the dog raises a paw and steps on the card – similar to when someone autographs a photo). I quickly took the card and asked the dog to pawtograph it; I then handed the card back to the man. He and his peers all lost it, laughing and thinking this was the best trick ever. This was clearly the highlight of their day and would become a story they would repeat to their friends. The news spread among their squad and the next day other firefighters came up asking for my dog to pawtograph their cards.

Incidentally, the trading cards were a big hit; oftentimes, requests were made for extra cards that the first responders could give to their children at home as well as display in the cabs of their vehicles.

When HOPE members met with another group of young women who had come to help, they were overjoyed at having a chance to pet the dogs. One said, "We have learned so much about what the people went through and we really appreciate the opportunity to help them." Another said, "I like giving back to the community."

One of the highlights of this deployment was a surprise visit by actor Rob Lowe, who was filming for the Ellen DeGeneres show. Upon arrival, he immediately wanted to meet his "namesake," a HOPE dog named Robby. He said, sitting on the grass surrounded by all 6 of the HOPE dogs, "Petting these dogs is my therapy." As he and the film crew left, he said, "I will be smiling for the rest of the day, thanks to these wonderful dogs."

Generally, HOPE deployments involve providing comfort and support for the victims of disasters, but this one was different. Although the first responders had dealt with a variety of crises in the past, few had experienced an event of this magnitude. Many of the first responders thanked us for being there. Every time we thanked them for their service and said that what we do is insignificant compared to what they do, they always responded with comments such as, "You have no idea how much this means to us and how important your service is." Witnessing the positive impact of our HOPE AACR dogs was an incredible experience and motivates me to help with the next disaster.

Discussion Questions:

1   Have you ever thought about working with dogs in a crisis situation? What might be some challenges to this type of work for you and the dog?

2   What qualities do you feel someone would need to engage in this type of service?

19 Providing Comfort to Flood Victims of Rural West Virginia

Sheila Consaul

In June 2016, rain began to fall in rural southern West Virginia. Far from a normal summer shower, the area surrounding White Sulphur Springs was quickly inundated by torrents of water that overtook the town and surrounding areas. Measured at nearly 10 inches of rain falling in just over a 12-hour period, the nearby river flooded, homes were knocked off their foundations, small buildings floated away and, sadly, 23 people lost their lives. It was deemed one of the deadliest floods in West Virginia history.

Fortunately, help arrived as soon as the rain stopped. Initially, the stunned but determined residents jumped into action along with the first responders, utilizing whatever they had available – personal pickup trucks, **ATVs** (all-terrain vehicles), and their bare hands – to search for victims, missing people, and pets – as well as ferry supplies such as clean water, food, and cleaning products.

As part of the response, HOPE Animal-Assisted Crisis Response (AACR) sent teams of specially trained crisis response dogs and their handlers to provide comfort to the victims, first responders, and family members left behind. Specially trained dogs have been used for years to provide therapy visits of all kinds to schools, universities, libraries, rehabilitation centers, and retirement homes. AACR, an advanced form of animal comfort, has been employed at such tragedies as mass shootings, tornados, hurricanes, fires, and civil unrest. In West Virginia, those affected by the massive flooding were happy to visit with sweet, caring canines, and their handlers.

As a HOPE AACR member, I drove from my home in Virginia 5 hours to southern West Virginia with my 4-year-old Golden Retriever, Lucy, to help. HOPE AACR partnered with the United Methodist Committee on Relief (UMCOR) as the local Emmanuel United Methodist Church was being used as a distribution center for food, clothing, cleaning supplies, and other humanitarian services.

DOI: 10.4324/9781003204534-22

Lucy and I were stationed at the Emmanuel Methodist Church greeting those coming for supplies, information, or simply comradery. While we were there, an older gentleman pulled into the church parking lot in a beat-up pickup truck. He walked toward the door wearing denim overalls and a sweaty T-shirt. His work boots were covered in mud that had splattered nearly to his knees. He came to the church for supplies, but before going inside, he saw Lucy and stopped. Not only did he want to pet Lucy, but he also wanted to talk to her. He bent down to look her right in the eyes and said "Hello, what's your name?" He chatted with her for a bit, not at all worried about the lack of a verbal response, and after a few minutes, continued on his way. Clearly, Lucy's presence brought him some peace and hope during a very difficult time.

In addition to spending time at the Methodist Church visiting with people and hearing stories of their loss and devastation, Lucy and I also walked down the hill from the church to the main street of White Sulphur Springs. While closed to vehicular traffic, a few people were milling about along the sidewalk – some doing whatever they could to help and others, frankly, still in shock. The shops and stores were all closed, many damaged by the flooding. The people we met while walking Main Street thoroughly enjoyed petting Lucy, watching her do tricks, and just engaging in anything that might take their minds off the incredible destruction of the community.

The next day, Lucy and I traveled to the nearby town of Lewisburg. There, a large relief center was set up in the high school gymnasium. The bleachers of the gym, which would normally be filled with students watching a sporting event, were piled high with cases of water, cleaning products, food, snacks, diapers, and other necessities.

Given that we were visiting a school, there were numerous children who came in with their parents or other relatives. Children naturally migrate to friendly dogs, and here was no different. One young girl, about 5 or 6 years old, beelined over to Lucy to say hello. Rather than the usual pat on the head, this young girl knelt right in front of Lucy's face. Despite the chaos of the flooding disaster and the buzzing of activity in the gym around her, the little girl began a very intense conversation with Lucy. As the little girl chatted away, Lucy listened intently in return. It was as if they'd known each other forever. Perhaps the girl was telling Lucy about her hectic and traumatic last few days. Or maybe she was asking Lucy what she thought of her visit to West Virginia. Frankly, I'll never know what the little girl said to Lucy, but I do know that for those few moments, Lucy gave that girl the special gift of love, kindness, and undivided attention that only a dog can.

Discussion Questions:

1 In the midst of a crisis such as a flood, fire, tornado, hurricane, or mass shooting, how well do you think dogs can provide stress relief and overall comfort to victims or first responders?
2 If you were personally affected by a disaster or crisis, would you like to have trained comfort dogs available to provide stress relief? Why or why not?

20 Magical Moments with Maggie

Yvonne Eaton-Stull

Maggie was a very special dog from the moment I picked her out. From a litter of shark-teethed pups jumping up on me, she sat behind the melee, staring at me with her big, brown eyes as if saying "pick me". I did, and it was the best decision! As an English Labrador Retriever, she was a very smart dog, learning quickly, enjoying life and loving everyone she met. These basic skills made for a great therapy dog, but her intuition was something that was magical. She knew who needed her most and made connections that I cannot explain.

Maggie had been a therapy dog for only a short time when something happened that made me consider whether she might make a good crisis response dog. I was presenting at a trauma conference and was asked to assist in a roleplay demonstration with about 30–40 other participants simulating an apartment fire. Usually, Maggie worked a room, starting where she entered, but this time she made a beeline all the way across the room to a woman sitting on the floor with her head in her hands crying. Maggie nudged her hands away from her face, kissed her and laid right in front of her placing her chin on the woman's leg. I thought to myself "Wow, this lady is a good actress" and I said, "she really likes you". The woman responded, "No, she knows this is too real for me. You see, I had a housefire". This roleplay was no simulation for this woman, and Maggie seemed to know. This is when I truly knew she had the skills to be a crisis response dog. Shortly after this conference, Maggie got certified with HOPE Animal-Assisted Crisis Response and became the first crisis response dog in Pennsylvania.

Maggie worked numerous crises, but her first mass shooting was in response to a request from the Red Cross to the Virginia Tech Shooting. This April 2007 shooting resulted in the death of 32 students and faculty and the wounding of 17 others. While we were providing support on the campus drill field, a young woman ran over exclaiming "That's my dog!" as she threw herself to the ground and embraced

DOI: 10.4324/9781003204534-23

Maggie. Apparently, Maggie looked remarkably like her dog at home. She sat with us for some time as she shared how other students got to go home and get support from their families, but she was unable to do so. Maggie comforted this student as she shared her emotions and experiences.

Upon return from the Virginia Tech Shooting, Maggie made a television appearance. A pre-school teacher viewing the news contacted me asking if Maggie could visit her classroom. She taught children with Autism. The teacher shared that one boy was non-verbal, and sometimes became frustrated at being unable to communicate and would bite his hand. I think she told me this so I didn't push too hard or ask him questions. Maggie and I sat in the room and one at a time, the children got to come and meet her. This particular boy seemed very excited to meet Maggie. He sat and pointed to her vest and looked at me. I said, "That's her vest". I swore I heard "vest" under his breath. Then he pointed to her tail and I said, "That's her tail"; he said, "Tail". The teacher spun around in shock and couldn't believe what she was seeing. We proceeded to play this game of him pointing, me telling him what part it was, and him repeating the word. Although this was originally a one-time visit, the teacher said she couldn't believe it and asked if I could please come back again. On only the second visit, this boy didn't just say a single word; he said a full sentence: "Read to Maggie?" I exclaimed "Yes, she would love that". He grabbed a picture book and began to point at things in the book and tell Maggie what they were. The teacher was in tears.

Finally, while working as a Counseling Center Director, I often received referrals for students with disciplinary concerns. One young man was required to see a counselor in order to be able to return to campus. He reluctantly agreed, stating "I guess I will see the one with the dog". This began a lengthy relationship helping this young man share his experiences of abuse and foster homes that had formed his views that the world was an unsafe place and people could not be trusted. One turning point in therapy occurred as he was sharing especially difficult memories and Maggie was asleep on her bed. I felt the mood change, and he lowered his head breaking eye contact with me. At that very moment, Maggie jumped up and hopped onto the futon next to him, kissing him and lying beside him, putting her head on his leg. He was able to continue this very difficult talk while petting Maggie and getting her support to go on.

It is these magical memories that make mourning Maggie more manageable.

Discussion Questions:

1 Do you think some dogs have special skills and abilities for crisis response work? Explain.
2 How might the support of a crisis response dog help an individual share their emotions?

21 Can Dogs Sense Stress?

Susan Herman

Can dogs sense stress? Science says yes, we hear stories how dogs knows when their owners are having a bad day, but what about with a stranger? Is your dog able to walk up to a stranger and indicate to you that this person is experiencing high levels of stress and anxiety? I believe some dogs are certainly capable of this.

I have two Crisis Dogs, certified with HOPE Animal-Assisted Crisis Response (HOPE AACR), who have spent countless hours giving comfort and support to people after a crisis. We have been deployed to assist after hurricanes, floods, student deaths and mass shootings. My dogs are able to sense stress and are drawn to the people who need them the most. They help by laying their head on the laps of these trauma victims and looking into their eyes or leaning against them as they sit together – offering them support and providing a way to help them process their emotions. I have been trained to watch the signs my dogs give and to let them work with minimal interference. Yet, nothing prepared me for the experience I had with my Leonberger, Talon.

Talon and I were deployed to assist after a mass shooting where, unfortunately, there were many fatalities. We were to be working in the Assistance Center along with other canine teams from HOPE AACR, interacting with people who had witnessed the shooting or had been in the store at the time of the shooting. There was a gentleman, Bob, who was a regular visitor to the Center. We spoke daily as he visited with Talon and the other dogs but all I knew about Bob was that he worked in the building where the shooting occurred. Talon had a fondness for Bob and really enjoyed his daily visits, including the extended belly rubs and scratches.

One day, Talon and I were going outside to walk "the wall". The wall was the fence that surrounded the business where family members and friends were leaving flowers, candles and memorials for those who died during that dreadful day. Bob asked if he could join us, and we

DOI: 10.4324/9781003204534-24

all headed for the steps. Bob was behind us and Talon would only go down 2 or 3 steps then stop and turn to make sure Bob was still with us. Bob and I joked for Talon not to worry, that we were not going to leave Bob behind. Talon continued stopping every few steps, looking back for Bob as we were leaving. I thought to myself, boy, Talon really likes Bob.

As we headed outside Talon took his position between Bob and I, leaning against Bob's leg. The wall is a very somber place where friends and families came to mourn and remember their friends and loved ones. We walked past people lighting candles, others were reading the cards and posters that had been hung on the fence. Some were talking quietly in small groups and others were standing alone crying. As we walked in silence Talon leaned harder against Bob's leg making him veer slightly toward the wall. Suddenly, without any warning, Talon crossed in front of Bob and sat, making Bob stop. Bob leaned down and petted Talon, telling him "Don't worry Talon, we will be okay, I am here with you buddy, we will be okay". After a few minutes, Talon stood, returned to his position between Bob and I and we continued to walk. As we continued walking, Talon again started leaning against Bob's leg and before long Bob was veering toward the wall. Suddenly Talon crossed in front of Bob again and sat. Bob bent down and petted Talon again, reassuring him that "We will be okay buddy, we will be okay".

I had never seen Talon do anything like that before. I had walked along the wall numerous times prior to that day with other people in crisis and Talon had walked along beside them like a gentleman. Yes, he would lean against their leg, but he never pressed so hard that it made them veer off their path and he definitely never sat in front of anyone, let alone multiple times.

Talon continued his process of leaning, pressing hard and then turning to sit in front of Bob – the entire way down the length of the wall. Each time Bob would lean down and pet him, repeating to him "It's okay buddy, we will be alright". When we got to the far end of the fence, we stood in silence looking at the parking lot. Talon was sitting between Bob and I, leaning against Bob's leg while Bob petted his head and stared across the parking lot. Finally, Bob started talking, pointing out where he was when the shooting began. He showed me where the shooter was and described in vivid detail how he moved along the parking lot shooting his victims. Bob had witnessed 11 people murdered that day. Looking back, I have no doubt that as we walked along the wall that Bob was reliving that day. I now understand why Talon acted like he had. I believe he sensed Bob's extreme stress and anxiety as he relived that day and stopped frequently to help Bob regain control. This was just one of numerous examples of Talon doing his job – offering support in his special unique way – connecting with Bob in a way only he could.

Discussion Questions:

1   What are possible welfare concerns for crisis dogs that may be different than those for other types of therapy dogs?
2   Have you had any experience in which you feel a dog displayed an intuitive sense? Please explain.

22 Challenging the Assumption of Who Needs Help

Batya G. Jaffe

I remember it was Tuesday, and it had been a difficult and tiring day. Lucy, my lovely Cavalier King Charles, sensed it and, as always, stayed right next to me. Lucy is not only part of my family, but she is my partner for work as an Animal Assisted Crisis Response (AACR) certified dog. AACR is a crisis response intervention that includes trained human-animal teams to provide support and comfort to individuals affected by crises and disasters.

Suddenly, I got a call from United Hatzalah's (Hatzalah means "rescue" in Hebrew) Psychotrauma and Crisis Response Unit. While living in Israel, I was the head of the unit's AACR division and an emergency was taking place for which they needed my particular expertise. Little did I know that the rest of my day would become an emotional tailspin.

The details on the call weren't clear – but the need for the Psychotrauma team was evident. I geared up and prepared Lucy who was already waiting by the door. I picked up two more responders and planned how we would proceed. Who would benefit from our services? Who from the three of us would take command?

When we arrived on the scene, we were not prepared for what we found. Usually, the type of emergency we respond to occurs in a single house or a single street; but this disaster area included the whole town. If you close your eyes, you can picture it. The roads were packed with police cars, ambulances, and firefighter trucks. All of the people in the town were gathered outside of the factory. To this day, I remember the stress level in the town – palpable; one could smell it. There was a thickness in the air; the day felt gray. Everyone was gathered together along the streets and houses, the whole area filled with dark, smoky air.

I parked my Renault, and we started walking. We were updated by the local crisis response team and understood the scene: there had been a fire in a fireworks factory, two young men were still trapped inside.

DOI: 10.4324/9781003204534-25

The fire had ceased by the time we arrived, but the scene was still full of smoke and glass; rescuing the young men was going to be very challenging.

At first, we thought of asking the groups of people outside to leave, go home, and allow the first responders to perform their job. However, Lucy changed our minds; she decided she had a more important task to handle. She pulled me to a bus stop where a teenager was sitting by himself. He looked despondent, just staring at the ground. Lucy went and stood next to him, but there was no response. Lucy brushed her head against his knee. Still, no response. But Lucy knew what she was doing, and I trusted her. She continued gentle nudging, and then it happened. The boy dropped to the ground, put his arms around Lucy, and started crying hysterically. After some time, the hysteria began to subside, but he continued to cry softly. He then shared that one of the trapped young workers was his best friend. After Lucy and I comforted him, a friend of his was able to approach and the young man was able to respond to his friend's support. Lucy had taken this young man through the bridge he needed to cross before he could connect to another human. We left him with his friend and continued to walk.

We came across a police officer and a firefighter deeply immersed in a discussion about the technicalities of the scene. They stopped talking the moment they saw Lucy. Lucy approached them and enjoyed their attention and caresses. While petting her, the firefighter turned to the policeman and asked him: "Do you realize we haven't taken a break since 6:30 am?" It was then 4:00 pm; they had been working for ten consecutive hours. "I haven't gone to the bathroom or eaten anything all day," one confessed to us. Coming to this realization, they decided it was time for a short break. Lucy had been able to distract these first responders from the stress they were under and give them an opportunity to take a break from the turmoil so they could re-prioritize their needs.

Lucy pulled me again. She wanted to approach a firefighter waiting for the order to go into the factory and begin the rescue efforts. I thought perhaps it was not a good time to approach him at such a crucial moment. But the firefighter thought otherwise. He kneeled down to Lucy and took off his mask. I could see tears welling up in his eyes. I didn't immediately understand what was happening. I started talking to the firefighter, and he explained that one of the workers trapped inside was his nephew. He had been waiting for hours in the sun and extreme heat, dressed in his full gear, waiting to go in and rescue him. I was doubtful about approaching the firefighter, but Lucy knew better, and once we had established contact, I was able to offer him emotional support.

After several long hours, we finally returned home. We had experienced a very complex scene, treating a large and diverse population. From kids to firefighters, Lucy once again proved how aware she is of what people need during these times of crisis. Together, Lucy and I were able to provide those affected with support and distraction, open bridges of communication, and offer methods for coping with the myriad of feelings they were experiencing.

Discussion Questions:

1 What benefits do you see an Animal-Assisted Crisis Response can provide in a scene as the one described?
2 How do you interpret the relationship and dynamics between Lucy and her handler?

23 The Washington Navy Yard

Ned W. Polan

The Naval Sea Systems Command occupies a five-story building that houses almost 3000 Navy and civilian employees in the Washington, D.C. Navy Yard. One morning in 2013, a subcontractor with a concealed sawed-off shotgun entered the building and proceeded to shoot at people throughout the building. There were 12 fatalities and 8 injuries before he was taken down 90 minutes later. It was feared that there were other shooters, so employees continued to shelter in place and the site remained locked down for the day.

Immediately, the Navy summoned HOPE Animal-Assisted Crisis Response (hopeaacr.org) to provide comfort and encouragement to the staff, many of whom had horrific personal eye-witness experiences that day. Brinkley, my golden retriever partner, and I arrived the day the Navy Yard reopened. On that first day, we were stationed with Navy behavioral health specialists at a site where people came to collect the belongings they hurriedly left behind at their desks.

This may seem like an impossible setting for a heart-warming story. But it isn't. The Navy observed that people really engaged with the dogs during quiet, private times. So, on our second day we were sent out unaccompanied. The Navy Yard is a beautiful park-like site on the Anacostia River, and on that second day many people got to laugh at the tough Navy squirrels who faced down golden retrievers and Bernese mountain dogs like curious little bulldogs! That was the first of many heartwarming surprises we experienced during the four weeks Brinkley and I spent at the Navy Yard over the following two years.

The dogs helped many people begin to talk about their feelings and experiences and to have some diversion from what had happened. It was a difficult time for all of us. But interactions with the dogs brought people into the present, into something pleasant, if only briefly, almost like instant mindfulness. There were many heartwarming events; the lasting significance of some became fully known to me only much later,

DOI: 10.4324/9781003204534-26

sometimes years later. Three weeks after our first week at the Navy Yard, at 4:30 am, a person texted:

> I first saw Brinkley when I returned to collect items... I was so pulled towards Brinkley and actually walked behind him to read his vest. I had no idea he was a service dog for us ... never did I think the Navy brought this type of team in. It was wonderful. I have a beautiful reminder with a baseball card of Brinkley that I keep on my dresser to see every morning ... thank you all for your support and love. Big hugs to Brinkley!

That person later remarked that they hoped to get their own dog one day.

Two years later, on the day the staff moved back into the completely renovated building, that person wrote again:

> I am forever grateful to you and Brinkley—he was such a comfort when I got to meet him ... we moved back into the building today and I still thought of that meeting. God bless the doggies. It is such an amazing program, and I am forever grateful. I now have a new puppy and she is my happy comfort, maybe one day she will be a comfort to others just as he is.

Now, eight years later, we still remain in contact—and they too have a Great dog!

Another person, who we saw every day at the Navy Yard, emailed me on the first anniversary of the shooting, at the exact hour of the shooting:

> I wanted to let you know how much you and Brinkley and all the other HOPE staff and companions did to help me during those following weeks. I leaned on the friendship and the love of all the canine visitors. They were so sweet, so patient, and so tolerant. I was able to silently share myself with them, look into their eyes and connect. That connection helped me make it through my day, during a time when there didn't seem to be too much to feel positive about. And I know that many of us at The Yard felt the same relief and love. Thank you, and Brinkley, and all your team for your good work.

Five years after the shooting, the facility commander, Brinkley, and I happened to all appear as speakers in an All Hazards Emergency

Preparedness Conference. In his keynote address, the Admiral introduced Brinkley and warmly remembered the unique value of that warm furry chin on his knee that day.

We truly receive amazing gifts from animals.

Discussion Questions:

1   Consider one of your own negative experiences. What calming, positive thoughts/memories can you attach to them?
2   How do YOU relieve stress after a prolonged stressful experience?

24 The Dog That Brought Hope and Brightness to a Challenging Christmas Season

Yahaira Segarra-González

In Puerto Rico, we like to think that we have the longest Christmas in the world. We start celebrating in November and it lasts until mid-January. Generally, this is a time of joy, family gatherings, and celebration. However, the Christmas in 2017, following hurricanes Irma and María, was more complicated. These hurricanes caused wide destruction and many families lost loved ones and struggled through the holiday season with no water, electricity, or stable housing.

These natural disasters caused long-term intense economic crisis, and even the Christmas of 2019 was challenging. Yet there was a sense of fighting for a better future in the country, and the feeling of joy that typically surrounds Christmas celebrations had returned. In our tradition, on January 5, many families symbolically go out to find grass for the camels of the three wise men, who on that night, it is told, arrive with gifts to the homes on the Island. Tragically, during the dawn of January 6, 2020, a 5.8 earthquake occurred in the southwestern region, followed shortly afterwards by a 6.4 aftershock. Thus, the fear, the pain, and the difficulties returned. However, the overflow of good-hearted intentions to help those who suffered the direct impact of the earthquakes was evident. My university sent us to the municipal shelter in Guánica, which was sheltering hundreds of families. We made several visits in those initial days, but one visit was exceptionally special.

I called a good friend, Emanuel, who has a beautiful Goldendoodle named Coral, and explained my wish to give emotional support to the survivors. Emanuel, who has experience with animal-assisted interventions, was happy to bring Coral and assist. Upon our arrival, several people approached us to greet Coral. We spent time talking with several people who were taking refuge there. One woman we approached was talking to personnel from an aid agency. When she saw us approaching with Coral, she mentioned that she wanted us to bring Coral closer. She began gently petting Coral and crying softly.

DOI: 10.4324/9781003204534-27

She shared that one of her dogs had died in the earthquake and she had been forced to leave her other dog at home. She explained that although her brother was caring for the dog, she desperately wished her dog could be there with her. Coral calmly remained by her side while she told us her story, and thanks to Coral, this woman felt comfortable sharing her concerns. She felt safe expressing the pain of losing one of her dogs in the earthquake as well as how much she missed her other dog. Her story made Emanuel and I think about how she might be able to be with her dog. We realized that many survivors were in similar situations; they did not have the kennels or leashes needed to safely bring their companion animals with them into the shelter. So, at the end of this visit, we had a new mission. In a couple of days, we returned. This time we came with the supplies necessary for these pet guardians to be able to bring their companion animals with them to the shelter. Again, there were tears, but this time, they were tears of hope and relief. Coral was the impetus of this effort. Through her ability to connect with these survivors, we were able to identify a need and work together as a team to make a difference. Our efforts were followed by veterinarians and other animal welfare organizations that were able to preserve the bond between numerous pets and their guardians.

Discussion Questions:

1   What difference can having a dog as part of a crisis response team make? Think about survivors' perception of the crisis response team.
2   What qualities should a dog have for this kind of work?

25 Sometimes Silver Linings Have Tails

Sandy Hook

Heather White

In 2012, a shooting occurred in a school in Connecticut that would be a defining factor in many people's lives. This shooting happened at Sandy Hook Elementary School and shockingly took the lives of twenty children and six adults in the school. At the time, I was working for a therapy dog organization and had been involved in crisis/disaster response through animal-assisted crisis response organizations for several years, so when the call came, I was ready. I chose a very special therapy dog and handler team to accompany me. We were sent to offer emotional support to the staff and students, some of whom had been in the elementary school when the shooting occurred. Training in National Incident Management Systems, psychological first aid, and experience deploying to natural and manmade disasters prepared us for what we could expect, yet the feeling of such loss and grief was palpable and raw.

Losing so many young lives in the blink of an eye is an unbelievably difficult thing to sit with. In coordinating some of the teams for this deployment, I was on and off grounds for the two weeks of the response, with each visit showing me the vast amount of support and strength within the community. Within the intense hurt were also moments that reflected the start of people finding some solace and healing.

Of the dogs and handlers I worked with, one team still stands out in my mind as a shining example of what it means to be a truly exceptional team with the highest level of skill and kindness and that was a handler who had a first responder background with one of the smartest, happiest, and fluffiest Australian Shepherd by his side. On the first day, we navigated connections and became familiar with the community. Spending time in one of the schools, this team brought with them safety, gentleness, kindness, and an opportunity to spend time in this space with those impacted by the tragedy. Countless children and school staff ended up spending time with this team. As the handler shared all about his teammate, Ronan, his furry partner, would show off his extensive

DOI: 10.4324/9781003204534-28

list of tricks, offer up a belly rub or two, and lean in for hugs and ear scritches, with many of the children leaving with a "trading card" (in essence, a transitional object and lasting memory of the moments they spend with this team). At the end of the week, I was again walking with this team through the school, when we came across some of the students transitioning between classes. As we chatted with them, they gave more ear scritches, and some jokes were cracked, a few giggles, and happy tail wags were had. The handler offered up a trading card to one of the children, a very quiet, more reserved girl who seemed to be clutching her books tightly to her chest as she reached out to pet Ronan. This girl shared that she already had gotten a trading card the first day that team had arrived, and she opened up her arms from around her books with the card held in her hand and said she had carried it around with her every day.

This truly touching response has echoed in me since that day. Providing a ray of light and kindness in a time when it's needed is a feeling that transcends species. A connection is a connection and when those positive memories and experiences are shared with individuals with and without paws, it can be even more special. This particular team had a wonderful knack for meeting each person where they were at, with the handler often sharing that Ronan was fantastic at keeping things to himself, and if children wanted to whisper into his ear what they truly wished, sometimes that can help. For the many, many people this team met along a therapy dog team career spanning several years, I am confident it did. Over time, people might forget what is said when visiting with a therapy dog and handler team, but they don't forget how the experience made them feel. This team brought unmeasurable gifts, including gentle strength and hope, especially during those visits to Sandy Hook.

Discussion Questions:

1 What are qualities you remember of experiences of those who have sat with you during difficult times in life?
2 What do you wish you could say to therapy dog teams who deploy to crises and disaster?

Part 4

Unique Settings

26 Assessment and Therapeutic Advancement through Human-Animal Interactions

Eileen Bona

I have been seeing Ashley for 6 months. The only reason she comes to therapy is because she is court-ordered to do so as part of her probation. Ashley is 14 years old and has made it clear she does not like therapy. She makes comments like: "All therapists are stupid. I hate people." Despite her negative attitude toward therapy, however, Ashley has shown up for most of her appointments, stays the full hour and talks about important issues in her life. I have a very loose, flexible therapeutic agenda for our sessions because I have learned that if I begin to act like "a therapist," Ashley will pull away; maybe even drop out. Ashley has been around the therapeutic block and I am her 10th therapist.

Yet, therapy with me is different because I practice animal-assisted therapy (AAT). The reason I choose to work with animals in my practice is because they are often effective for helping to bridge the gap with children and youth who are hard to reach or resistant to engaging in the therapeutic process. So far though, my attempt at including animals into my sessions with Ashley had not gone well. Ashley claimed to be allergic to cats, didn't like my black lab dogs and explained she felt too cold to work outside with the horses. I was at a loss.

I truly believe that everyone wants help. I refuse to believe that people are happy getting in trouble at home, at school or with the law. I hoped that somewhere deep down inside, Ashley was coming for reasons other than a court order. I continued to try by letting her direct our sessions and allowing her to carry out her court-ordered obligations with me, even though she was sometimes less than pleasant, and our hour sessions often seemed to last a lifetime for both of us. Then one day, Ashley did something profoundly brilliant. She asked if she could bring HER dog to our session.

After consultation with her mother, confirming that the dog was safe, healthy and had up to date vaccinations, I agreed to meet her dog. At first, Ashley insisted on many rules that had to be in place if her dog was

DOI: 10.4324/9781003204534-30

to stay. For example, my cats had to go, my dogs were not allowed in and I was not allowed to touch her dog. In an attempt to try something new with the hopes that it would work, I agreed. It was an immediate marked change. Through her interactions with her dog, I got to see a loving, flexible, understanding teenaged girl. She did not get angry when her dog didn't listen to her, she set firm and assertive healthy boundaries and she showed much appropriate affection to him when he sought it from her. Ashley appeared to have wonderful social skills with her dog but when interacting with people helpers and her mother she was rude, hurtful, aggressive and volatile.

Ashley continued to bring her dog to therapy sessions. As time progressed, she allowed her dog to sit with me for the duration of the sessions. At first, she would try to get him back but when he wanted to stay, she eventually allowed it.

In our session last week, we could see my two black labs begging to come in with their big brown eyes. It was cold outside. I said nothing. Ashley said "I think they want to come in." I said: "Only if you want them to." I had been wondering if Ashley had empathy outside of her own dog for some time now. "Yes, please let them in. But I don't like big black dogs, especially labs because they are not fluffy." I let the dogs in and my 7-year-old Thorpuppy went right over and laid down next to the couch Ashley was laying on. I told her I would move him. Surprisingly, she said: "No, that's ok." Thorpuppy lifted his head and peered into her eyes, their heads were almost touching. Ashley reached out and began to stroke his head. Thorpuppy let out a big sigh and so did I. Ashley looked at me and said: "Maybe I don't hate all big black labs." I silently rejoiced. Ashley's biggest obstacle is her inflexible, all-or-nothing thinking. Thorpuppy may have just helped her to begin to understand the necessity of learning to accept and compromise.

I wasn't sure it was possible with this challenging young woman, but, yet again, I saw the power of the human-animal bond as it created an avenue for me to reach a client and help her build upon the skills she needs for a healthy life.

Discussion Questions:

1   What concerns might you have about a client bringing in their own dog?

2   How might you use the empathy Ashley showed toward her own dog to help her develop empathy toward people?

27 Charley the Bulldog and Her Visits with Incarcerated Youth

Taylor Chastain Griffin

There was something so unique about the way that Charley, the bulldog, walked through the doors of the Youth Detention Center for her very first visit as a therapy dog in that setting. It's not an easy place to visit, even for us humans. You step into a world within a world – one with its own set of rules, echoing noises, scared children, guards, and locks. It takes a very special dog to thrive in this context, let alone to win the hearts of the young people who are so often and so understandably closed off from everything, including positive human-animal interactions. But as Charley entered that facility for the first time, she seemed utterly unphased. Whereas I would typically use a treat to encourage a new dog as they walk through the metal detector, Charley strutted right in – chest poked out and crooked tail wagging. She was undistracted by the clanking gear hanging from the staff. Instead, she remained focused on locking eyes with them, plopping to the ground for rubs as soon as a smiling face looked her way.

Walking into the youths' living spaces with Charley was a much different experience than making an entrance with some of my smaller, fluffier therapy dogs. The kids immediately had questions about where she came from and why she had scars and other physical abnormalities. They sat quietly to hear her rescue story, gently placing a hand on her hip when I assured them that although it was broken in the past, she was healed and free of pain now. Though there would be moments of solemnity when they would listen to the hardships that she'd overcome, Charley wasn't one to allow the room to stay serious for too long. She'd snort, show her belly, or nudge a hand to bring the child back to the moment – back to play and to affection. That's just how she was, even on the day I first met her after she was brought into the vet by the good citizen who found her – starved, injured, and close to death. Even then, her primary posture was to wag, connect, and survive.

DOI: 10.4324/9781003204534-31

Charley went on to visit Youth Detention Centers all around the state, forging friendships with countless young people who would report that her walking through the door was the best part of their week. Kids who just moments ago held the stature of a restrained adult shed the weight that was on their shoulders, coming to the ground to sit criss-cross applesauce so that Charley could do her best to squeeze into their laps. I was always amazed at how during these informal sessions the youth would start to demonstrate such care for one another. Whether it be by proudly showing a new member of the community how Charley best liked to be pet or by calling over to a peer who they knew was having a hard week: "Hey, come talk to Charley, she'll understand." I often did nothing more than be quiet and watch the interactions during these visits. Having studied psychology for years, I stood in awe of the allyship that was so quickly created between these kids and this very special dog. A sense of kindred survivorship was palpable in the environment, forming an invisible tether between the hearts of these children with the therapy dog who they'd sometimes only meet a handful of times. More times than I could count, I would hear them say things like "You've been through hard times, and you overcame. So will I." Or "People weren't good to you when you were young, but you still know how to love. I'm just like you, Charley girl!"

I learned so much about the way to care for others and for myself by watching Charley share the gift of her love with the world. She seemed to notice absolutely nothing about a person that would make them different or cause pause in forming a connection. She was truly excited to greet all who crossed her path. She was fully present in all moments – thoroughly enjoying treats when it was time to have one, snoring in relaxation when prompted to rest, and bringing others back to present moment through her sweet gaze and playful pawing.

Charley's incredible testimony for loving the world was a lifeboat for me when it came time to navigate the grief of her passing. I'd often sit and visualize the millions of little moments she had with the people she visited, each connection rippling like water in a stream to yield more and more love. Charley's cheerful focus on each new person she met was not because of aloofness or lack of discernment. Instead, it was because when she looked at a person, I truly believe she had a way of seeing the best possible version of who they were. Her endless tank of positive regard influenced her ability to overcome the odds, and it permeated each one of her interactions as the brilliant therapy dog that she was. I've come to love the old expression "Be the person your dog thinks you are," although that's a very high standard when it comes to imagining Charley's perception of me. It's my mission now to keep her love going and to show the world how much goodness can come from sharing our lives with animals like her who teach us so much about the healing power of love.

Discussion Questions:

1   What unique traits about Charley did the young people at the Youth Detention Center connect with? Why do you think they were often more attracted to her as compared to other therapy dogs without a rescue story?

2   Charley had a way of inspiring people to live in the moment. How do you notice the animals in your life encouraging a sense of presence?

3   Charley was the queen of unconditional positive regard. How can we show this gift to the people we work with?

28 Jude and Letty

Sarah Deering

My name is Jude. My Mom adopted me from the Humane Society when I was just a puppy, and then I grew really big! She always says I have *the sweetest* Labrador face, and that she wishes she knew what else I might be mixed with. I work with Mom as a certified co-therapist helping young ladies at a therapeutic group home find healing from the awful things that have happened in their lives. I get to see a lot of miracles, and this is one of my favorites.

Visit One:

Today I met Letty. She didn't make noises and was different from the other humans I meet who smell strongly of feelings. Letty is bigger than the other humans, and she had trouble moving quickly or keeping her eyes open. She smelled like old food, unwashed person, and other bad stuff. I didn't mind, because I like investigating new smells. Letty brought a food bowl into the room where we talk about all the feelings, and when Mom started to talk Letty began to fall asleep! I don't think Letty meant to snooze though because she spilled some milk. I was happy to lick it up for her and Letty squealed when I licked her hand. She even let me clean off her face. I think we're friends now.

Visit Two:

I showed my friend Letty all my tricks today. I love doing that with new friends so they know how cool I am! Mom gave Letty a bag of treats and told her what words I understand. Letty didn't use the words but she liked my tricks, so I started doing them all at once. Except then I got flustered because I like when things follow an order, and Letty wasn't giving me commands. I gave Mom calming signals and she told

DOI: 10.4324/9781003204534-32

Letty I was anxious without the words. Then Letty asked me to "Sit." Everyone was SUPER proud of me for doing it. I'm a good boy.

Visit Three:

It's been lots of days since we saw Letty, but man was she excited to see me today! I remembered her too and had all the wiggles. We went outside and Letty helped Mom give me a bath. Mom talked about how to scrub out my smelly areas and why soap is so important. I hate soap because it gets rid of all the smells. Once we were done, I got to play with the hose water and Letty laughed a lot. I love when my friends laugh.

Visit Five:

Today Letty didn't smell as much like old food or dirty human. But she wasn't happy, and this made me sad. Mom told her I'd been waiting all week for a walk, so Letty put my leash on even though I don't think she wanted to. While we were walking, I heard Mom ask Letty if she wanted to talk about school. Letty yelled something and Mom's eyes got big because it was the first thing Letty had said since "Sit." It didn't surprise me because I hear all kinds of things all the time; I just kept walking and everyone followed me. Mom smelled nervous and said some things to Letty. I know some of them were questions because her voice did that weird thing at the end. Letty didn't speak again today, but she still answered Mom the way I do, without "words-words." They both seemed to feel better at the end.

Visit Seven:

When we got to the house, Letty was already dressed for a walk, so Mom got my leash and we set out. Mom and Letty weren't talking, but then suddenly Letty exclaimed, "He's looking for his family!" Mom asked Letty a question. When Letty answered, I smelled Mom's heart break. Then we all felt what Letty felt, what she was holding on to. I'm good at holding on to feelings, so we stayed like that for a bit. Mom and Letty talked more until Letty was crying super, duper hard. I nudged my head into Letty's hand so she knew I could help with these kinds of things. Letty petted me softly, and then we all walked back. *Letty gave me the BEST hug before she went back to her room.* Then Mom told me I was the Best Boy. Which, I am.

From the Author ("Mom"): "Jude and Letty" is based on our work with an adolescent female who had been trafficked by her mother in infancy and removed from her family's custody in before age 3. "Letty" was then sexually abused in multiple foster homes, finally bonding herself to a much older male who sold her in exchange for cash and drugs, all before she'd even hit her teenage years. By the time she arrived at our therapeutic group home, she didn't or couldn't speak, and her violent and/or sexual outbursts were escalating. Letty's weight made her intimidating, and her lack of verbal cuing made her rage episodes appear spontaneous. She'd previously bounced between treatment homes with a lack of continuity in care, resulting in her being heavily over-medicated, arguably out of fear of what she might do if not sedated. When Jude and I met her, Letty had been "nonverbal" for ~2 years and was diagnosed (and medicated) for Autism Spectrum Disorder, Oppositional Defiant Disorder, Attention-Deficit Hyperactivity Disorder, Post-Traumatic Stress Disorder (PTSD), and anxiety. Our work was short-term in nature, so I don't have the ending to her story, but I can tell you that in less than two months of working together, Letty was grooming herself appropriately, greeting others, forming positive connections, and her prescribed medications were significantly reduced. She could hold conversations and attend school and was making tremendous progress in combatting her PTSD symptoms.

Discussion Questions:

1   What happened during those first seven visits would not have been possible without Jude as my partner therapist. How do you think his perspective and/or attention toward Letty altered the dynamic from a traditional therapeutic setting with only humans?

2   During Visit Seven, Letty remarked on Jude's behavior, offering a projection. If you had been leading that session, what might your response have been to help Letty address her defense mechanisms?

29 The Life of a Strong and Caring Therapy Dog in the Canadian Prairies

Colleen Anne Dell (with the assistance of David Brock Batstone)

It is commonly said that we grow up tough in the Prairie Provinces of Canada, forced to deal with the harsh elements – the scorching heat and tornados to frigidly cold temperatures with dumps of snow. It is also said that we are kind people, willing to give others 'the shirt off our backs' when in need.

I think the same is true of dogs in the Prairies. Let me tell you about the life of Kisbey, a strong and caring Boxer who was born on September 14, 2007 in the town of Weyburn, Saskatchewan, Canada, just a few hundred kilometers from her namesake, the town of Kisbey.

As a young pup, Kisbey was impulsive and strong-willed. If she sniffed the scent of a bath or bedtime in her imminent future, she had a knack for escaping from wherever she was at. In fact, so much so that we started calling her Kisdini, after the great escape artist Houdini! She was also physically strong, keeping up with a dirt bike ripping around the yard in her younger years or jumping high into the air to catch the Frisbee that she loved so much. She would literally push furniture to find a piece of kibble that dropped behind it. Kisbey also liked to cuddle and show affection when her Boxer energy abated. We decided to see if she would like to volunteer as a therapy dog, and that's when her characteristics shined through the brightest. I don't remember anything too eventful happening during the therapy dog test, but I do clearly remember our very first therapy dog visit. It was at the Regional Psychiatric Centre in Saskatoon, run by Correctional Services Canada. Bringing a therapy dog to visit was a new idea for the facility and that first appointment they had us waiting an hour to visit with the participant. Finally, the buzzer rang, we heard the harsh clank of the door unlock, and the prisoner, Jordan, was standing in front of the window that separated us.

And then Kisbey and Jordan saw each other – Jordan started to grin from ear to ear and Kisbey began her Boxer wiggle. The door opened

DOI: 10.4324/9781003204534-33

and Kisbey was all over Jordan. I think we broke every therapy dog rule. Kisbey danced around Jordan in circles, licked her all over, and kept puppy bowing to get her to play. I was unprepared for Kisbey's over the top reaction to Jordan, but it started to make sense when Jordan said that Boxers are her favorite dog and she had not seen one in person for over a decade. Jordan was not even 30 years old and had been incarcerated since she was a teen.

About 10 minutes into the visit, Jordan asked me if I thought Kisbey knew she was 'a good person'. Before I could answer, Kisbey flipped on her back for some belly rubs. I told Jordan that this was a sign that Kisbey completely trusted her, even though she just met her. This made Jordan very happy and was the start of a very special relationship between her and intuitive and caring Kisbey.

A few months later, Kisbey met Alex, another prisoner at the Regional Psychiatric Centre, and her strong-willed personality again paid off. Alex, too, had been incarcerated for more than a decade, and because of his psychiatric illness, he was often very subdued and not present 'in the moment'. Well, Kisbey was having none of that. After greeting Alex in her typically exuberant way (but having learned to follow the therapy dog rules by now), Kisbey was persistent in asking him to engage with her. No matter how dissociated Alex was, Kisbey would try her best to get his attention. Sometimes I would give her a toy to help her efforts. She would drop the toy at his feet, pick it up, drop it at his feet, and so it would go until he picked it up and played with her.

I remember this one time though that Alex shuffled into the room and immediately laid on the cold floor. Kisbey didn't do any circles that time, didn't try to engage him, she just went right to him and laid on the floor beside him. I was speechless for the entire duration of the 20-minute visit. Something very similar happened with Jordan on another visit. Kisbey just knew what Alex needed and adapted easily from an exuberant playmate to a gentle and caring companion.

Kisbey was a therapy dog for 9 years, doing in-person visits, all the while sharing her caring and strong personality. She visited everywhere from prisons to university classrooms to homeless shelters. This even continued during the COVID-19 pandemic as we shifted to virtual visits.

When Kisbey passed earlier this month with my partner and I by her side, and I turned to leave the veterinary clinic, I had a strong urge to return and ask to see her one last time – so I did. I needed to thank her for all she has done in her lifetime for others, including me and my family. It is an honor for me to tell a small piece of Kisbey's life story.

The lasting legacy I know she has left in peoples' lives and hearts was her ability to communicate that she cared in an honest way, and to use her strength to do what she wanted and needed to do with fortitude and determination.

Discussion Questions:

1 What qualities do you think a therapy dog might have that humans are less likely to display to the same extent?
2 Do you think that prisoners may respond differently to a therapy dog in comparison to another human, and why?
3 Do you think there is anything humans can learn from therapy dogs about using their intuition in their interactions with other humans? If yes, what would this be?

30 Animal Therapy in a Hospice Setting

Caryn Friedlander

I started volunteering with hospice in 2003, after my husband had fully recovered from a bone marrow transplant. Walking alongside him through his treatment and with the deep uncertainty of a life-threatening illness, I recognized my capacity to be present for others who are facing their own mortality or that of a loved one. Hospice work is a rewarding practice where, to some people's surprise, there is much to learn about life. A few years into volunteering, I also discovered the benefits of doing this work with a dog by my side. I visited a patient who adored dogs, so I brought along a really sweet pup I was dog sitting. When I entered the assisted living facility with Agave, the entire atmosphere brightened – everyone in the lounge smiled and wanted to meet my buddy. I immediately knew that one day I would do this with my own dog.

Tashi, a giant Goldendoodle, came to live with me at the age of one and a half. His early training had been spotty but we caught up on things, and by the time he was three he was ready to have a go at being a therapy team. He's clearly got what it takes – besides his new name, which means 'hello!' in Tibetan – he's intelligent, loves all beings, is lively but knows when to chill, and is tolerant of high emotional states and kids' hugs. We trained and registered with Pet Partners, and began to work at our inpatient hospice.

We had been volunteering a couple of years when we started visiting Tom, a young man in his thirties who had an incurable glioblastoma. Tom's mother was there daily, and his many siblings visited from across the country over a period of several weeks. They all loved dogs, and Tashi was delighted to interact with everyone. Tom, though bedbound, was still oriented and animated during his first weeks at hospice, and Tashi would sit by the bedside so that Tom could pet and talk to him.

DOI: 10.4324/9781003204534-34

After spending time with Tom, Tashi would check on others in the room. When people respond to my pup, he often sits close to them, facing away in hopes of a back rub. When they stop petting him, he immediately swings his big head around and gives them a hopeful look, clearly asking them to continue. It always gets a laugh and more love.

As Tom's disease progressed, he went from being interactive, to sleeping more frequently, to 'active dying', which is characterized by a coma-like state and long pauses in breathing. During most of our visits, Tom's mother would be by his bedside, touching her son frequently. The last time I visited, when Tom was actively dying, his mother was sitting on the daybed, about eight feet from her son's hospital bed. With many patient families, this would seem normal. But with this family, as I entered the space, I immediately felt the physical distance between mother and son. I tapped on the open door, and Tom's mother smiled and invited us in. We went and sat beside her, Tashi between us and leaning into her leg. She and I spoke softly while she stroked the dog.

Like most dogs, Tashi is quite sensitive to energy, and is generally drawn to the more active people in a room. In a hospice setting, with patients who can't move or talk much but might still benefit from some animal therapy, it can sometimes be challenging to direct Tashi's attention toward the patient. However, on this day, after sitting beside Tom's mother and enjoying a good rubdown, Tashi suddenly got up and went directly to Tom's bed, stretching his leash – and my arm – to their maximum lengths. Nothing I could see had changed with Tom's body or breath, but Tashi was very intent in his movement toward the bed. I looked at Tom's mother and said perhaps I would say hello too. I moved to the bedside and told Tom that Tashi and I had come to visit, and how much we had enjoyed spending time with him and his family (hearing is thought to be the last sense to go, even when someone is unresponsive). Soon, his mother got up and went to the other side of the bed. She stroked her son and decided to give him a massage. She had some lavender oil, and as she gently massaged his arms, his chest, and his legs, she mentioned how much Tom loved to be touched when he was a child. We stood there, on either side of her son's failing body while she told me stories about his life. It was such an intimate, sacred moment; I was deeply honored to be there. I don't know what Tashi saw or felt, but it was clear that he had brought us all into the moment, by Tom's bedside, where the connection was tender, real, and deep.

Discussion Questions:

1   What are the benefits that an animal can offer within hospice settings?
2   What precautions should be implemented before bringing a therapy animal into a hospice setting?

31 In Sickness and in Health

What Dogs Teach Us about Life and Death

Rachel Hogg

It is mid-March and summer, here in Australia, is over. We are celebrating Linda's birthday with forced lightheartedness, defiance overlaid by a desire to pass this off as "just another birthday". We know this will be her last birthday, but we do not know that this is the last full day of her life. I have brought Eddie, my Australian kelpie, with me, and although he is not the stock image of a therapy dog, I hope he will lighten the atmosphere and draw our attention away from death, if just for a moment.

My relationship with Eddie is complicated. I grew up around dogs, and my career has been fueled by a lifelong interest in animals, yet if it is true that we are defined by the most fractured relationships we have, Eddie has brought me to my knees. I love him, and he is well-cared for, but I am often my worst self with him, and I know it. The discomfort of this is heightened by my background studying human-animal relationships, and the irony of this is not lost on me. Neither is the juxtaposition between what I believe animals are capable of and the ways in which Eddie's inexorable, relentless nature rankles me. A chasm seems to exist between the dopamine-enriching therapy animals in clinics and the dog in my own backyard destroying his fifth bed in two months while I attempt to teach a statistics class on Zoom during the pandemic.

Dogs hold a kind of deity status in animal-assisted therapy circles, as well as in the "pet" stratosphere. We look to this species to humanize us and enrich our lives, and never more so than during the pandemic – when pet ownership rates soared. What is often lost in these benign narratives of harmony and companionship, however, is the real complexity of these relationships. Eddie and I are not unique in our uneasy truce, trying to find our co-existence blueprint. But in this moment, there are bigger things to worry about. My friend is dying. Dinner draws to a close; Linda is exhausted and as her partner, Rod, wheels her away from the dining table, I retrieve Eddie from the backyard. As we

DOI: 10.4324/9781003204534-35

enter the house, Linda is sitting nearby in her wheelchair. Eddie, usually bubbling with excitement, sits back on his haunches. He is silent, still, almost reverent, looking at the woman in front of him. I have never seen him like this; suddenly we are all quiet. He moves toward Linda and crouches down, licking her feet.

Linda is a neuropsychology academic with what should have been a sparkling career ahead of her, the brain cancer diagnosis coming approximately six months after earning her PhD. Linda loves her pet bird, Phoenix, but she is not a "dog person". And yet, for a few seconds, her face changes. Eddie moves forward and begins to lick her outstretched hand. He does not see cancer when he looks at her the way we, her human companions, cannot unsee it, our fear and hers combining. It is as though being with Eddie in this moment has created a container for her consciousness where things fall and land more lightly, a softer version of reality opening up in front of her and drawing her forward, transforming "what is" into something altogether less threatening than living with death on your shoulder.

Watching Eddie sit quietly at Linda's feet that night, a transposed version of himself, makes me both uncomfortable and proud. Uncomfortable that I undersold him, and proud of him for showing up like no one else could. In the days that follow, Linda is suspended in time, caught in a state of conscious not even the medical professionals seem able to label or describe in definitive terms. Euphemism and cliché quickly color our engagement with death, even before the dying has begun. I ask the palliative care nurses if Eddie is allowed on the ward and they say, "Sure, absolutely fine", even though one of them is scared of dogs. There are moments when I ask myself why I am doing this and whether it is fair to him to bring him into a hospital. He is not timid; I am not worried that he will be overwhelmed by the emotion of the moment or the foreignness of the hospital environment. But suddenly he seems like a resource that we can tap into to step out of ourselves as time quickens and slows, both variations painful in their own way.

In the months following Linda's death, I return to the question of Eddie's therapeutic presence, a presence embedded within two contrasting realities, simultaneously inhabited. One of unknowing, an insouciance contingent on the absence of spoken language, coupled by an irreverent disinterest in the distractions of society. The other reality, one in which Eddie met Linda, is of deep knowing; the ability to strip back human defenses and make life at its truest more visible, visceral, immediate. Perhaps, here lies the therapeutic power of dogs. They are sensitive to human suffering and uninvested in its causes.

Discussion Questions:

1　In Linda's last hours of full consciousness, Eddie had the capacity to momentarily lift her out of one reality and into a more open, unbounded space. Is this therapy? Is "therapy" in its truest form a fluid construct, the lines between professional and personal encounters blurred not just by context, but by the nature and form of the human-animal interaction that takes place?

2　Does an animal's power lie in part in their separation from us and our human meaning-making capacities? Or do we love dogs because they allow us to see ourselves in them? Simply put, do we find them therapeutic because they are like us, or because they are not like us?

32 "Steven" and Shannon

Amy R. Johnson and Melissa Potts Kutchek

He came in dressed in khakis, dress shirt and tie, "just in case"; just like he did every day. Sixteen-year-old "Steven" was tall and husky and looked like a football linebacker. But Steven did not like football; in fact, he liked Thomas the Train. A lot. He could tell you everything there was to know about Thomas and his friends. Steven was chronologically 16 years old, but cognitively and emotionally, he was closer to 6 years old. He could barely write, could not read, had tactile issues and did not engage well in conversation. His early years were tragic – including multiple foster home placements where he was severely abused and detrimentally neglected.

Steven is not the type of youth we would typically see in the Teacher's Pet: Dogs and Kids Learning Together program. Teacher's Pet is a program that typically pairs at-risk youth in juvenile detention and community mental health settings with harder-to-adopt shelter dogs for a 10-week intervention. However, sometimes programing can be tweaked, and special cases are welcomed.

Initially, Steven was reluctant to work with the dogs. He was leery of most dogs and was afraid of pit bulls. While interacting with the dogs, he would not remove his tie, even for safety reasons, because "you should always look nice…just in case." *Just in case* meant in case he had a visitor…which he rarely had. The facilitators had to work around his need to keep on his tie while ensuring his safety.

The first day, Steven was introduced to all five of the dogs participating in the session. One of the facilitators stood with him to ensure the dogs did not jump up on him or otherwise make him uncomfortable. Shannon, a gray and white pit bull, caught his attention. And Steven caught her attention as well and she moved toward him to say hello. He crouched down to say hi in return and she ran over to him and put a paw

DOI: 10.4324/9781003204534-36

on each shoulder and licked his face. Steven laughed and shouted "She's hugging me! She loves me!" For a kid who had not experienced much love throughout his life, this moment was pure gold.

After each training session, the youth are asked to write in their journals about their work with the dogs (how they felt, their progress, their frustrations, etc.). Steven had minimal writing ability but managed to write "I love my dog Shannon." This was his first ever structured sentence! The teachers, facilitators, staff all cheered him on.

Shannon was very active and had not yet learned any cues or manners; but she was very smart and absolutely loved to snuggle with her humans. When she was with Steven, it was like she knew that he needed a slower, quieter version of herself, so when with him, she was calm and often curled up next to him or in his lap to snuggle. Steven loved the focus drills as Shannon caught on quickly and welcomed, Steven's excitement followed by a good snuggle. But most of the time, Steven would simply sit on the floor with her, read to her, tell her all about Thomas the Train. After 6 weeks in the program, Shannon was adopted. Steven was sad, but felt excited for her, and a tad envious that she was going into a loving home.

Steven took on a new dog, continued writing in his journal and participating in the class. Upon completion of the program, not only did Steven's writing abilities improve, but his ability to focus had improved. He learned how to train Shannon with basic behaviors. He learned how to calm his emotions and outbursts a bit more. He could actually hold a conversation and participate in class, giving answers to the question of the day. He became more involved with his peers. He even read a few sentences from the presentations, and by the end of class, he wrote multiple sentences in his journal, on his own!

After the 10-week session ended, the facilitators went to visit the boys on Christmas Eve. Steven was very excited to see them and immediately took them to his room to show them his Thomas the Train collection. The facilitators also saw a collage of pictures on the wall next to his bed and displayed prominently was the photo of Shannon hugging him. He said to them, "I loved her and it makes me happy to see her when I wake up every morning!" One facilitator had to walk away because it touched her heart so deeply, she began to cry. Steven's story touched everyone.

The possibilities of a human-animal bond are clearly endless, and often unexpected. There is no barrier of language in a human-animal bond because the universal language of love is truly spoken by the heart.

Discussion Questions:

1 What similarities come to mind between Steven and Shannon and how would those similarities contribute to the mutual human-animal bond?
2 If you were a facilitator, what strategies or techniques would you have used to help Steven foster growth?

33 Comfort during Crisis

Angela Moe

In February of 2016, my community (Kalamazoo, Michigan) suffered an unfathomable tragedy. An Uber driver went on a several-hour killing spree, murdering six people and critically injured two others. There were no connections between the incidents or victims, nor any clear motive. The victims included a young mother who survived multiple gun shots while shielding children at her apartment complex, a father and his teenaged son who were looking at cars at a dealership, and four retired ladies who were leaving a restaurant along with an adolescent girl (who survived). Kalamazoo is a small urban hub in southwest Michigan; it seemed everybody knew or had a connection to the incident.

It took two years of legal wrangling for the case to go to trial, and in that time additional resources were deployed to serve the community. Through a fortuitous set of connections, my therapy dog, Sunny (a Golden Retriever, two years old at the time) and I were contracted to support the relatives and friends who came into town for the trial. While I have crime victim advocacy experience, providing direct support alongside a fairly young therapy dog on a case of this scale was an entirely new prospect. We were told that many of the families were "dog people" and that we were cleared to enter the courthouse and a hotel staging/respite area, but beyond that, I did not know what to expect.

The morning of the trial, and unbeknown to the families, the killer pleaded guilty to all charges. Everyone was caught off guard and clearly frazzled as they were ushered from the courthouse to the hotel after the plea. Our work quickly shifted from sitting with relatives watching a live stream of opening statements, to accompanying nearly 100 grieving family members to a debriefing with the prosecutor. While some were thankful to be spared the trial, others were angry at having been robbed of the opportunity to observe the proceedings and/or testify.

DOI: 10.4324/9781003204534-37

I will never forget the solemn procession down the escalators to this meeting, though I was preoccupied with trying to find the right balance between showing solemn respect and a willingness to engage. As I've since learned from working with Sunny, I need not have worried. He acknowledged each individual, his warm brown eyes and softly wagging tail indicating care and concern. The changes were palpable – sunken shoulders straightened, frowns turned to grins, and tears slowly evolved to light laughter as Sunny gently patted his front feet in anticipation of making new friends. As is so often the case with therapy dogs, their very presence connotes safety, acceptance, and unconditional love.

Throughout that afternoon and the following days, Sunny's eagerness to sit with anyone who needed him never wavered. However, his most poignant interactions occurred with young people. One in particular was the teenaged niece/cousin of the slain father and son. As we passed her table during that first meeting, Sunny caught her eye. She discreetly slid off her chair and settled with him in the middle of the floor. I gently dropped his leash and stepped away. With her head bent over Sunny and her long blond hair shielding them from the outside world, the two shared something very personal and necessary for several moments. As she stroked Sunny's fur I could see her shoulders shake as the tears arrived in a torrent. As is so often the case with deep grief, especially amongst youth, words are impossible and inadequate. That's the thing about dogs. They understand just from our demeanor. In this way, Sunny offered a loving respite to the most vulnerable in the room.

Similar interactions occurred that afternoon and in the following days, as folks rearranged travel schedules and left for home. On one of those days, Sunny accompanied a grief counselor to an impromptu therapy session with a young child whose mother had been injured at the apartment complex. The girl was struggling to make sense of everything, not understanding why her mother remained so upset. Having recognized that she enjoyed interacting with Sunny, the counselor invited her to join Sunny in a corner of the large banquet room, and the three sat for nearly an hour. Sunny remained solidly at the girl's side, gently nudging her and keeping her grounded in the present.

A month later, most of these folks gathered again to witness the killer's sentencing, during which one representative for each victim presented a statement to the court. Those who had depended on Sunny earlier knew they could again, and did not hesitate to seek him out. We maintained contact with several of the folks we met during this experience. Sunny was proud to be invited to the high school graduation party for the girl he comforted at that initial meeting, reveling in the "good boy" praise after their connection was explained. He is prouder still to have been the inspiration for her acquiring a puppy she hopes to train as a therapy dog. One never knows the path healing will take.

Discussion Questions:

1   What do you think gives dogs the ability to comfort and support people during tragedies?
2   What are other settings for which therapy dogs like Sunny could be utilized to comfort victims of crime?
3   What types of skill and aptitude do you think the handlers of therapy dogs in settings like this need to have?

34 Regaining Memories with the Help of Jaime

Anna K.E. Schneider

How can you reach people who don't recognize their closest family and sometimes not even themselves in the mirror? Dementia is a challenge both for the patients as well as their families and caregivers. In the dementia ward of a hospital in Erlangen (Germany), numerous women and men are cared for. While some are more cognizant than others, many spend their days staring into nothingness; each one of them struggling with the same diagnosis of memory loss.

Together with my dog, Jaime, I participate in one of the animal-assisted therapy programs at a hospital in Erlangen. It is there that I was able to experience and share in numerous touching moments when patients rediscover a part of themselves through their interactions with an animal. Jaime, a six-year old black, medium-sized mixed breed, had always shown a particular affinity for human contact and we started our volunteer work in the hospital after completing the necessary training program.

In general, all of our visits start in the same way. The hospital staff gather a small group of patients in a room and seat them in a circle. The number of participants is limited, as is the time spent there since the interactions with the patients can be quite challenging. Patients may behave unpredictably, suddenly moving frantically or shouting. Even without such episodes, the work we do as an animal-assisted intervention team requires a great deal of mental strength and energy.

The patients in the ward take part in the therapy sessions for a variety of reasons. In some cases, they express a clear desire to participate. Other times, they are primarily unresponsive and the medical staff include them in the hope that the interaction may prove stimulating. The human-animal interactions are remarkably diverse. Some patients reach out, trying to connect to the therapy dog physically from the start of the session. At times, they need assistance as they are unable

DOI: 10.4324/9781003204534-38

to establish contact themselves. It is noticeable how much any form of physical contact means to the participants.

In cases of dementia, it is common to observe physical impairments in addition to memory loss. One objective of our sessions is to encourage our patients to use their hands, reach or grasp for things, and generally engage in touch. For this, having a soft-furred dog around helps immensely.

One of the male patients, "Jake" did not like to use his hands. Jake's movements were shaky, so he tended to keep them still in his lap and left the staff to take over any necessary tasks. He was, however, particularly fond of Jaime and enjoyed having Jaime pushing against him, sniffing him, or laying his head into his lap. Jake often made comments about Jaime's demands for his attention and seemed flattered by the dog's insistence. Over time, Jake would try to respond to Jamie's requests for attention. It started with the smallest movements, fingers twitching, when Jaime's head got close to his hands until he would start using his whole hands to give Jamie the requested pets. He would often comment about his shakiness, but it was clear that this didn't matter to Jamie. The delight in these interactions was clearly visible on Jake's face.

Sometimes, the tactile impression alone stimulates the patients to share stories. They may remember their childhood dog or recall surprisingly specific memories of encounters with other animals. While otherwise mostly unaware of their hospital surroundings, these interactions sometimes also prompt conversations about their patient status and current living situation.

Occasionally, it takes several sessions until patients want to interact. However, over time, most participants overcome their feelings of anxiety or intimidation and want to join in. As a result, they seem to enjoy the interaction even more and I have often observed a noticeable increase in their confidence. The experience seems to allow them to forget their patient identity – even if just for a moment.

One example of such an interaction is especially memorable. A female patient, nearly 90 years old, had been visibly wary of Jamie in previous sessions. She had kept considerable distance between herself and the dog and refrained from physical and verbal contact. Over time, as she finally chose to participate in the session, she appeared to overcome her anxiety and her behavior changed significantly. Over the course of the encounter, the reservations she had shown previously vanished and, in addition to tactile and verbal engagement, she went so far as to get out of her chair and join the dog on the floor (much to the consternation of the staff, whose concerned remarks and offers of help she ignored as she crouched on the floor to interact with the dog). For the duration of the encounter, it appeared that her fear of judgment and insecurities shifted into the background. What remained at the forefront was a moment of joy.

Implemented with care for the welfare of all involved (including the dog!), encounters like this confirm the potential of implementing animal-assisted therapy in the treatment of dementia patients. Watching patients reengage with the world through their interactions with Jamie is what keeps me coming back; knowing that together, we can bring moments of joy and connection.

Discussion Questions:

1   Which ethical guidelines are essential for training and working in animal-assisted therapy?
2   What are the limitations of animal-assisted therapy and when should caretakers or institutions refrain from using it as a treatment?

Part 5

Children, Young Adults and College Students

35 The Gift of Comfort

Sue Burlatschenko

As a large animal veterinary practitioner of many years, I have seen numerous instances of profound human-animal interactions. Certainly, we would be a lesser species if we were not able to enjoy the relationships we have with animals, be they large or small.

Along with being a veterinarian, I have become a relief foster parent, as my children have all grown and left home. This means that I spend a weekend with a foster child to enable the foster parents to have a small break. My first relief child, Rebecca, had fetal alcohol syndrome. I was uncertain as to how the first weekend would work out, and she was very nervous as well. Fortunately for me I have two bullmastiffs, a mother and daughter. Stevie and Lulu are the sweetest dogs and adore children, which is natural in a good bullmastiff. They took care of the problem for me when we were preparing for the first evening ritual of pajamas and a snack. I found Rebecca curled up happily on Stevie on the rug, and Lulu sitting right next to her. She clearly felt safe and loved, and the dogs did their part by staying close to her – somehow sensing her uncertainty and giving security with just their large and quiet presence.

At every visit, they welcomed her gladly, and she was thrilled to go for walks with them, holding the leash with me. They eased her into the new routine of staying at my house once a month, accepting her just as she was and in their own way giving her confidence. She always talked about them when she returned to her foster parents.

As we grew more comfortable with each other, I would take her out occasionally to light farm calls. I work with a pet pig sanctuary, which takes in unwanted or unloved Vietnamese pot-bellied pigs and gives them a forever home – unless an appropriate foster home comes along. These pigs range in size from 40 lb to 300 lb. They are grouped in small pods according to their personalities and how they get along with each other. The sanctuary currently holds about 150 pigs. The pigs are well socialized and enjoy scheduled visits with folks who want to

DOI: 10.4324/9781003204534-40

see what they are like. One day I brought her there, thinking that she might enjoy something a little different. We walked around with the owner, who I had called ahead and given some background. The owner had been a special needs teacher and was perfect for our visit. As we walked amongst the pens outside, the little girl was enchanted with one group of smaller Vietnamese pot-bellied pigs. They were essentially a group of 'teenagers', full of fun and curiosity. We went into the pen and she promptly sat down on a log. One particular pig, George, seemed to connect with her and sat beside her as she chatted away to him. Pot-bellied pigs are funny because their hair on the neck will piloerect (stand on end) when they are happy. George had a full-on forest of hair standing up and was wagging his tail madly. The little girl and George spent a long time together that spring day in the sun and it was difficult to have to break the spell to leave.

Although this is a simple tale of a girl and the animals that she met, the more intriguing part is the certain animals who chose her companionship. Much like people, animals seem to have a better sense of humans in need, and they become the unquestioning, voiceless witness to these lives. Yet animals are like people – only some exhibit this tremendous resonance with particular humans and many prefer to live their own lives separately. To have the positive impact of this connection happening between animals and humans is indeed a marvel and a reminder that good does exist.

Discussion Questions:

1 How do you think the interaction with George impacted Rebecca?
2 Have you witnessed examples where animals seemed to intuitively know what a person needed? What happened?

36 Beignet and the Class of 2021

Kate Drescher

Beignet is …

"A soft, caring, floppy face … comforting, loving … fluffy, gentle, understanding …emotionally aware, warm … sweet, welcoming, the happiest in the room" (quotes from those who have met Beignet).

In November 2019, I began a professional partnership with a Golden Retriever named Beignet who would change my personal and professional life forever. Beni (as she is often called by her students) is the embodiment of unconditional love. She was raised by two women who embraced her gentle spirit, fostered her desire to connect with others, and provided a safe and stimulating environment for her to develop into the amazing service dog she is today. Knowing her many gifts would allow her to change the lives of those she encountered, they made the ultimate sacrifice to share her with me to support the children with whom I work; children in need of love, validation, and encouragement.

I am a clinical psychologist in a K-12 independent school of approximately 450 students. For many years, I wanted to work with a canine to support my students' social, emotional, and academic development. When Beni came into my life, I knew I had a partner like no other, one who would have a profound impact on the students with whom she worked. However, what I did not anticipate is that Beni's presence would touch the lives of my community, lifting spirits and bringing joy to all.

Beni was trained by Canine Companions, and she knows approximately 40 skills that most service dogs have mastered to assist their handlers. However, her well-developed skillset is not what makes her so exceptional. It is her intuitive nature and ability to make everyone in her presence feel seen and heard that makes her the most popular staff member in the school (or at least that is what I have been told by the students). Beni is both playful and easygoing, a rare combination. She is as much at ease resting quietly beside a child who is learning to read

DOI: 10.4324/9781003204534-41

as she is engaging in playful interactions with students at recess who are practicing their social skills.

She had an especially meaningful connection with one student who found peace and acceptance in her presence. She knitted Beni a beautiful turquoise scarf and often said she was her favorite "person" at school. Her mood brightened noticeably (and almost immediately) in Beni's presence and Beni always met this student where she was at any given moment, providing her with the kind of personalized support she needed to feel settled. I often marveled at how Beignet intuitively knew what she needed and anticipated her every move.

Shortly after Beni's arrival on campus, I also noticed many other children, adolescents, and faculty began to visit my office, asking to spend a minute or two of time with her. This would often lead to introductions and impromptu conversations between students who did not know each other previously and were brought together by Beignet. They would often sit on the floor with her, scratch her neck, or ask for hug, one of her many skills! Her presence was also requested at faculty and staff meetings. When we were walking past classrooms, I would hear students enthusiastically say, "There's Beignet!" However, it was the positive effect she had on the graduating Class of 2021 that was most surprising and heartwarming.

In addition to being a psychologist, I'm one of the advisors for the twelfth graders. In that role, I greet them every day and serve as a point person for academic, social, and emotional issues. Beni accompanied me to my advisory meetings and classes and, in doing so, developed a deep, reciprocal bond with the members of the class who collectively experienced many stressors associated with COVID-19 and its aftermath.

Every morning upon our arrival to school, Beni would immediately head to our classroom to greet "her" seniors with a slow wagging tail and one of her favorite toys in her mouth. In return, they would shower her with praise and high-pitched compliments about being such a "good girl." She was also the recipient of more belly rubs than I can count! She would visit each of the three senior classrooms every morning, stopping to pause for everyone who expressed interest in spending time with her. On more than one occasion I would overhear the seniors saying she was the bright spot in their day. I loved seeing the older students in our school revert back to being young children in Beni's presence.

Fitting for their close relationship, the Class of 2021 requested Beni's presence at their graduation ceremony to support them in bringing their high school journey to a close. She spent time with them backstage to help calm pre-ceremony jitters and she sat patiently (and attentively) in the audience while they gave their speeches and said their farewells. While Beignet was often the one to initiate hugs with her students, on that day, the students initiated the hugs, of which she was the recipient of many. Beni supported her students to the very end, and I could not have been more honored to call her my partner. She continues to touch the lives of students and faculty in my school in big and small ways with her tenderness, openness, and unconditional love.

Discussion Questions:

1   How do you think the connections Beni formed with the students could have helped them cope with school related challenges?
2   What are some of the characteristics of Beignet that make her so well suited to the kind of work she does?

37 Teletherapy Dogs

Adam Duberstein

During my third year as a doctoral student, I completed a practicum in a private practice where I primarily worked with children. My supervisor assigned me the case of Timothy, a six-year-old boy who struggled with school, making friends, and had several fears that his parents described as 'unusual'. Timothy had extreme reactions whenever there were thunderstorms, he had fears of the dark, and he was mortally afraid of animals. Although his family had an elderly dog that he loved and did not fear, Timothy feared all other animals, ranging from spiders to mice to lizards to any other dog.

When Timothy was an infant, his toddler sister suddenly died of a genetic ailment while sleeping in her bed. This death shook the family greatly, and even though Timothy had no memories of his sister, he talked about her frequently. He often stated that he was afraid to fall asleep because he did not want to die in his sleep as his sister did. This fear manifested in Timothy having to share a room with his nine-year-old brother, because Timothy refused to sleep alone. His fears during the day were equally intense.

Timothy and I had only met for a few in-person sessions when the COVID-19 pandemic struck in March 2020. At that point, many people were gripped by fear and Timothy was no exception; his anxieties worsened during this time. As a psychologist in training, I had never before conducted telehealth, and I was unsure how telehealth from my home would go, especially because I have two rambunctious pit bull terriers who would likely be playing in the background while I worked with clients.

During the early days of the pandemic lockdown, my dogs were acclimating to me being home more frequently and I tried to get accustomed to working in an online environment. To me, teletherapy proved to be a blessing, as it allowed me to continue working in a field that I love

DOI: 10.4324/9781003204534-42

without curtailing my needed practicum hours. To my dogs, however, teletherapy was not quite so exciting. They appeared to wonder why I spent hours upon hours ignoring their pleas to play as I talked into a mysterious box. Then, the unexpected occurred, and my dogs began to engage with clients.

I was about halfway into a teletherapy session with another client when her dog started barking. In return, my dogs barked, and the session could have quickly devolved into a barking contest; however, the client was intrigued that I had dogs, and she asked if she could see them. I tend to be fairly reserved, so at first, I hesitated, but then I agreed. The client had been talking with me about relationship issues that were causing her a great deal of emotional pain; it was a difficult topic to discuss, but when she saw my dogs, she laughed and smiled. The dogs seemed to cause her to feel a bit of relief in an otherwise stressful, painful moment.

Informed by my earlier positive experience with my adult client's reaction to my dogs, I decided to introduce Timothy to my 'friends', Malka and Adina, who also happened to be dogs. I explained that the dogs would do their best to keep him safe from some of the things he feared – like storms. Somewhat nervously, he met them virtually. The dogs approached the camera enthusiastically; they were excited and happy that this child was paying attention to them. From that point on, something shifted and the dogs began to join me while I worked. I think, from their point of view, that the 'box' I spoke to frequently took on a new meaning, and people like this somewhat shy child existed 'in' this box. The dogs became accustomed to the sound of Timothy's voice, and I am almost certain that they knew that he had his sessions with me on Thursdays at 3:00 pm for, like clockwork, that is when they would wander in and join us.

During one of our sessions, Timothy shared how thunderstorms scared him. I explained that Malka, too, has a fear of thunderstorms. In another session, he talked about his sister's death, leading to a discussion about when Adina lost one of her newborn puppies. Another time, we talked about Timothy's fear of dogs. According to Timothy's parents, he feared their neighbors' large dog even though the dog was harmless and gentle. I explained to Timothy how Malka, who is part Mastiff, weighs a whopping 115 pounds. We also discussed how Adina's perceived ferociousness just means that she is ready to play. We talked about how his neighbors' dog was gentle, kind, and playful, like Malka and Adina. By the time our work together concluded, Timothy's mother reported that he no longer was afraid of the neighbors' dog.

Malka and Adina still join me for virtual therapy sessions, demonstrating nearly daily their ability to act as instruments of healing, health, and protection.

Discussion Questions:

1   In what ways did the dogs help to decrease Timothy's fears?
2   How did the virtual environment impact the ability to include the dogs in Timothy's treatment?

38 The Power of Prince William

Patricia Flaherty-Fischette

Prince William was a "senior disabled" pug in a Staten Island kill-shelter. The organization, Boxer Angels Rescue, saved him the week before he was supposed to be "put down" and loved him while also searching for his forever home. Miles away on the north shore of Long Island, an Irish American young woman was dealing with a recent suicide attempt by engaging in several different treatment modalities to deal with her sexual trauma and eating disorder. While transitioning to a different level of care (from in-patient to day-program), her treating psychiatrist suggested the idea of adopting an animal. At the time, she had left law school and was living at home, cared for by her family with very little independence (understandably so, given her mental and physical state). Her life centered around going to treatment and while she recognized the privilege to have that opportunity, she also felt lonely and numb. While she was learning (and re-learning) how to approach her body, feelings, and coping strategies, her psychiatrist recognized that she still had an extremely negative and self-punitive cognitive framework. Her treatment team suggested that adopting an animal could be an opportunity to experience the unconditionality of love from an "unbiased" being (since she was convinced the people who *had* to put up with her were not reliable sources to assess her self-worth). In her mind, her loving parents and partner's unconditional acceptance and support were unreliable. She felt that they did not truly understand the evilness that existed inside her. So, with the support of her treatment team and family, she started looking at dog adoption sites.

This process was the first thing outside of her eating disorder that prompted any motivation. She had always loved pugs – she loved their smushed faces and adorable mugs – so she started searching for pugs. At the time, since she was living with her parents in a supportive

DOI: 10.4324/9781003204534-43

home, the treatment team agreed that adopting an animal would be safe for the animal as it would be a group process. She came across a picture of Prince (formerly named Alex) and the look in his eyes just resonated with her. She said that she saw in his eyes the same type of desire to be seen and loved that she also craved, and she knew they were meant to be. Prince William (named after her first true love as a tweenager) became her transitional object. He helped her feel okay as she started to explore more independence. She would walk with him, and it helped her become more mindful of the present moment. His interest in smelling something new or his refusal to walk one more step helped bring mindful awareness to the choices one has in life – the choices she had in life. She shared that Prince William would snuggle into her legs to sleep and, from the first night, slept in bed with her. He helped her slowly appreciate touch and, in time, learned to enjoy it again. She would feed Prince William each day and, over time, this ritual helped reduce her own anxiety about feeding herself. His enthusiastic curly tail wagging in anticipation for his food, his gleeful snorts as he gobbled down his food, and his confident swagger after completing his meal without judgment helped model for her what mealtime could be. She began eating while Prince William ate and found his soft fawn fur to be regulating as she pushed through the anxiety of each bite. Over time, she found it easier to eat because she was more interested in other things. She started writing for an animal advocate blog. She was able to work a few hours in the local library. Her world expanded beyond just her eating disorder.

She said Prince William didn't judge her for restricting, hurting herself, or using old behaviors to deal with intense feelings. His unconditional love provided her with strength. His love helped her challenge the old architecture (that, in time and willingness to explore in therapy, she learned to appreciate was developed in response to trauma) that kept telling her that she was bad and, therefore, deserved to be punished. She looked at Prince and all that he endured in his life, and he did not respond to his maltreatment by feeling unlovable. Instead, he was extremely willing to give and receive love. Prince William helped her tolerate the idea of an "ever after" – one that was happy *and* sad, scary *and* fun, and one that allowed for healing, the ability to love (both herself and others), and access strength she didn't know existed. Her Prince passed over the rainbow bridge several years later, but his gifts keep on giving; helping her achieve a happily-ever-after founded in safety, healing, confidence, love, and strength.

Discussion Questions:

1   For her treatment team, what was important to consider when suggesting adoption of an animal?
2   What themes emerged when she talked about the impact of Prince William?

39 Mickey Mouse and Lyn

Tara Harvey-Gros

The air was warm and breezy as Ann and 5-year-old Lyn walked hand in hand to pick up a couple of items from the store. Ann had been avoiding shopping with Lyn, but this would be a very short trip. Ann winced as she felt Lyn's hand begin to tighten. Lyn began to hum. Ann moved forward determinedly. Shortly after entering the store, Lyn's sensory overload began to escalate. The moving vibrations from the fluorescent lights were unbearable, the smells from vegetables and fried food and pastries, people moving and talking; more and more input invading her senses. Lyn tried her best to remain calm. She knew her mother wanted her to "be good". Yet, too much input, unbearable, no way out. Lyn went into gradual then total meltdown. She lost control. She threw herself onto the floor, began banging her head on the floor, screaming loudly, writhing her arms and legs uncontrollably. Her mother, Ann, knew what to do. Keep Lyn safe from herself and others, it was the only thing left to do. Shoppers in Walmart passed by and passed judgment – what kind of mother would allow her child to throw a fit like that? Other shoppers offered to help, not knowing what to do. Ann was extremely embarrassed, yet only wanted the best for her child. Unfortunately, these events were all too common.

At her daycare, ignoring the other children, 2-year-old Lyn ran into the room, making a beeline to snuggle with the stuffed dog in a corner. Ann noticed the other children laughing and playing together. She remembered her pediatrician telling her, "Don't worry, she will outgrow it" at Lyn's 1-year-old checkup. Ann had voiced concerns that Lyn was very fussy, did not make eye contact when taking a bottle, had difficulty sleeping at night, and did not hold on with her arms and legs when being carried. Ann would later learn that these were all classic symptoms of autism. Lyn received a diagnosis of autism at 3 years of age, having missed more than 2 valuable years of early intervention. Ann was both angry and sad when she realized the significant loss for Lyn.

DOI: 10.4324/9781003204534-44

Ann is single mom and Lyn is the center of her life. Although her wages are low, Ann considers herself very lucky to have a job at the school. This job enables her to work hours that accommodate Lyn's needs. One of these needs is ongoing occupational therapy. A primary goal for Lyn during these therapy sessions is to learn self-regulation skills. To teach this skill, her therapist, Tara, will introduce very small problems or manageable frustrations into her play. Over time, Tara will slowly dial up the problems and frustrations. Sometimes Lyn's occupational therapy sessions went well, sometimes they did not. Today, sitting in the lobby of the therapy center, Ann listened.

Ann knew this therapy session may be tough because Lyn had a bad day at daycare today. She could hear Lyn humming and stomping as she was escorted to the therapy session. Ann could hear that Lyn was gradually escalating. Then, silence. Ann thought, "What on earth just happened?" Ann slowly and quietly made her way toward the therapy room. Lyn's therapist, Tara, was on the floor with her. Lyn was belly down and in total meltdown, screaming and flailing her arms and legs. Tara looked up to see Shauna – a registered animal-assisted therapy volunteer, and Mickey Mouse (a small Shih Tzu registered therapy dog) standing at the doorway. Shauna is a dedicated volunteer who has witnessed first-hand the power of the human-animal bond many times. Her caring soul shines most when she is rescuing animals and volunteering with a therapy dog.

Both Shauna and Tara know that the safety of the animal is a top priority in animal-assisted therapy. Tara hesitated and considered the situation while Shauna waited for instructions. Mickey Mouse, meanwhile, looked happy – excited to visit with anyone.

After careful thought, Tara told Shauna, "You may have to go find another patient to work with but let's give this a try". Shauna walked Mickey Mouse toward Lyn very slowly and cautiously. Both Tara and Shauna were on high alert in case they needed to act quickly and remove Mickey Mouse. Tara nudged Lyn in an attempt to shift her attention toward the dog. Once Lyn finally noticed the dog, she immediately fell into total silence and began to smile. Both therapist and volunteer continued with great caution as Mickey Mouse moved toward Lyn. Lyn wrapped one arm around Mickey Mouse as he lay down with her. Lyn's face was one of pure bliss as she snuggled with Mickey Mouse and starred into his face. Mickey Mouse leaned into Lyn and relaxed. It was at this moment that Tara and Shauna looked up to see Ann standing at the door – with tears of happiness running down her face.

Discussion Questions:

1   What do you think it is about animals that make them of benefit when working with children on the autistic spectrum?
2   What are the welfare implications for animals such as dogs that are highly sensitive to sounds and smells?

40 Compassion through Canines

A Boy and a Dog

Laura Hey and Mary Jo Powers

Hard to believe it's been so many years since my life took a drastic change for the better—all because of lessons I learned from a dog!

In elementary school, I was a "frequent flyer", meaning I was sent to the principal's office virtually every day. Managing my anger and getting along with others were not in my repertoire! I'd been in special groups before to help me with these problems. We'd had discussions, watched videos, and practiced good social skills through role-play, but none of those things really helped. See, I was fueled with a lot of pent-up anger. I started altercations with kids and teachers at school, and with my family; often. In third grade, my school counselor asked if I'd like to be in a group of boys working with a dog. That sounded fun to me since I like dogs—except for the other boys in the group. We were all very active, reactive boys and could not get along. But the idea of working with a dog won... I agreed to join the group.

The "Compassion through Canines" group used activities with a therapy dog to help us develop better communication skills, behavior management, and positive interactions with others.

The dog for our group was a German Shepherd named Savard. As soon as we met, Savard and I connected. I immediately loved that dog! Savard's handler and my guidance counselor told us boys that we'd need to be nice and could not have any outbursts or aggressive behavior if we were to be part of this group. Savard's handler explained the importance of interacting with Savard in a way that demonstrated respect and care for him. We learned that how we behaved would influence Savard's feelings and behavior, as well as the people around us.

Lots of lessons stood out to me in that group because of Savard. For example, like me, Savard had the strength and size to be pushy or mean, if he wanted to be. Unlike me, Savard had a gentle and kind demeanor. But amazingly, as the days went on, my positive behaviors grew! As

DOI: 10.4324/9781003204534-45

a group, the other boys and I grew individually and together. We had created a positive bond with Savard *and* each other.

One day, we had to try to get Savard to knock over ten plastic bowling pins, set up like in the game, with a tennis ball. We'd learned how to direct Savard in a kind voice to do specific behaviors (sit, come, etc.), and the importance of praise when he did what was asked. So, we boys listened to each other's ideas, took turns, and came up with a great strategy. We got Savard to knock down every pin by picking up and then dropping the tennis ball right over the targets as I called him to move forward. Wow!! The other boys and I praised Savard, then actually congratulated each other for a job well done. We were getting along and learning to work together as a team! We even stood arm in arm after our great success and asked to have our picture taken!

Another activity that was cool was "Savard's Resume". In reading and discussing Savard's resume we learned that although he was a kind, happy, and loving German Shepherd, Savard was not perfect. Most importantly, his imperfections did not make him a "bad dog". After we talked about Savard's "good and bad" qualities, each of us boys had to reflect on our own personalities to complete our own resumes. It was easy listing my weaknesses and negative qualities, but I needed *a lot* of help to come up with positive things about myself. However, after I'd finished, I had a whole different perception of myself, realizing that despite my issues and challenges, I wasn't a "bad" kid. In fact, I even had some really good traits, like leadership and a great smile!

As my positive social skills and good character developed, my self-respect grew. The other boys and I had begun this program as very separate, antagonistic individuals possessing some highly challenging behaviors. We left the group *as a group*; a group of respectful peers who supported one another and had experienced our own gentler, nurturing, and compassionate sides.

My new friends and I were so proud of our accomplishments that we asked to share our experiences with our peers. We got permission to do a presentation to our classmates, describing what we'd learned about positive behaviors and interactions with animals and people. I was able to proudly proclaim, "I don't fight anymore! Savard doesn't have to; I don't have to". My trips to the principal's office stopped, and I still carry Savard's lessons with me and apply them throughout my life.

"Savard is my hero—he literally helped me change my life forever! Savard taught me that there's a better way to behave. Thank you, Savard. You were a wonderful friend and mentor." (Sentiments expressed by Wyatt Caldwell, now 24 year old, for the dog and program that "changed my life").

Discussion Questions:

1 Why do you think the therapy dog helped these children change their behaviors, when fun games, role-play, and videos could not?
2 Would incorporating a different size or breed of dog have had the same impact on this group of boys?
3 What other types of shared experiences, aside from animal-assisted interventions, might create similar outcomes?

41 I Can Listen Like Indy

Terri Hlava

When Indy was about three years old, long before her younger brother, Pakuna, was born, she began visiting Mrs. Adnil's classroom for children with communication differences. The children were diverse in terms of ages, backgrounds, first languages, and specific communication, social, and academic challenges. Indy, their canine classmate, provided species diversity as well. Besides participating in daily learning activities, Indy rode the school bus and accompanied her classmates on fieldtrips.

In preparation for a fieldtrip or a class visitor, Mrs. Adnil would ask students to explain one way that Indy showed respectful behavior. Then she would ask the students how they could show respectful behavior like Indy, expressing the expectation using Indy's conduct as a model that students could emulate. "Indy sits quietly, so we can…," Mrs. Adnil would begin, her voice trailing off, inviting student involvement. "Sit quietly!" the children would shout. Then Mrs. Adnil would hold her index finger to her lips, bend slightly forward at the waist, and whisper, "Indy sits …, so we can sit …," and the children would whisper "quietly" with their index fingers pressed against their lips while I held my finger to Indy's lips too. When Mrs. Adnil would ask the students to stand up, Indy, as a member of the class, would stand too. Then, when Mrs. Adnil mentioned "sit," as in, "Indy 'sits' quietly," everyone would sit quietly, including Indy. "Why do we need to sit quietly when a guest is speaking?" Mrs. Adnil would ask. "So we can listen!" a child would shout as Mrs. Adnil hinted by tapping her ears, leaning slightly forward again. "And who always listens carefully?" she would ask. Invariably, a chorus would rise, "Indy listens carefully," and Mrs. Adnil would add, "so we can …" "Listen carefully!" the students would respond enthusiastically in unison. When it was time to demonstrate listening carefully, I gently lifted the tips of Indy's long Labrador ears so that she could hear better as Mrs. Adnil and the students cupped their own ears in turn.

DOI: 10.4324/9781003204534-46

Indy was the first therapy dog certified to work in an Arizona public school, and her students' success earned her a Governor's Award for Service to Students with Diverse Abilities. But that's not how we know that Indy made learning meaningful for her friends. After all, awards come and go, but learning must stay with someone to have a measurable impact. So, how could Indy claim to have such an impact?

Notoriety from that award brought a photographer and a newspaper reporter to Mrs. Adnil's classroom. Yes, this story happened back in the pre-cell phone era when photographers used film cameras and newspapers were delivered to front porches, not inboxes. Now, fast forward several years when Pakuna and I were out shopping and we unexpectedly met one of Indy's former classmates as he was retrieving a package of paper towels for a grateful customer. One of Indy's oldest and dearest friends, whom we hadn't seen in more than ten years, was working at the local grocery store.

When the customer left, I asked Christopher if he had attended Desert Sun Elementary School, and he said "Yes." Then he asked me if I used to visit there with a black dog named Indy, and I said "Yes." I introduced him to Pakuna, Indy's younger brother, and assured Christopher, when he asked, that Indy was fine at home. Then he remarked about the weather on that sunny summer afternoon and said that, "Indy might not like it to be so hot today." Pakuna and I agreed with his explanation for Indy's choice to forego the shopping trip. And then it happened…

As he knelt down and stroked Pakuna's downy-soft ears, Christopher said to me,

> Tell Indy I love her and that I still have her picture by my bed. My mom put it up for me. We taped it to the wall so I can see it every night and morning. I can listen like Indy. I still can. Tell Indy I love her.

I said I'd tell her and I added,

> Christopher, I know just what picture you mean! Indy still has it by her bed too! It's the picture from the newspaper when you two were both at Desert Sun! She's kissing your face, you're petting her cheeks, and you're wearing a red sweatshirt with long sleeves, right?!

Christopher's quick smile flashed fond recognition as he said, "That *is* the one. Please tell Indy I still have it too, and I look at her every day. I love Indy!" I told Christopher that Indy saw his image every day in that same picture and that she loved him too.

As soon as we got home, I called Mrs. Adnil and told her about meeting Christopher, and she told me that he and some of his former classmates were enrolled in community college courses starting in the Fall. She said that they all remembered learning with Indy. Now, that is lasting impact.

Discussion Questions:

1   How would you integrate a therapy dog into your own curriculum?
2   How would you measure the success of your therapy dog program?
3   What do you want to look back on after a few decades in the field, and what steps are you taking today to reach that goal?

42 Aksel to the Rescue

Elizabeth A. Letson

Hey Liz, it's Jana. I've thought about you and how you've helped me through all the time we shared. I'd really like to thank you personally and have you meet my son. I think about Aksel and your horses and I really wish I could see you again. Sorry if this seems "out of the blue" but you're the only therapist who has ever helped me. I really appreciate it. Hope all is well.

This message was in my inbox in 2020 and Jana (not her real name), who I hadn't seen since 2014, is now back on my schedule working on building a better relationship with herself and others that is based on healthy communication, trust, and respect.

As an Animal-Assisted Counselor, I incorporate animals, mainly horses, dogs, and cats, into my therapy practice. In 2014, while still working as a Youth & Family Counselor at a local nonprofit, I made weekly visits to a charter school to counsel a handful of high school students. My coworker and therapy dog was Aksel, a Saint Bernard with a beautiful coat of brown, black, and white fur, huge puppy-dog eyes, and a gentle, patient manner.

On a cool spring day, Aksel (175 pounds of pure joy) and I entered the charter school to meet with students for on-site counseling. When we walked in, 16-year-old Jana was the first student to approach us. Sensing something was off, I invited her to join Aksel and myself in my office down the hallway. After some small talk, she began to open up about feeling down and depressed, sharing details about the depth of her despair. Jana had a history of exposure to violence in her home and had experienced sexual and emotional abuse over the years. The extensive childhood trauma had taken a significant toll on her mental and physical health, leading to symptoms of depression, anxiety, insomnia, and post-traumatic stress disorder.

DOI: 10.4324/9781003204534-47

Eventually, she completely opened up to Aksel and me, with him lying quietly on the floor, as she sat beside him. The evening before, Jana had reached a very low point and had attempted to end her life. Thankfully, the attempt failed, and her life was spared. Before her mother and siblings got home, she had "pulled herself together" and didn't share her suicide attempt with her family.

With the support of Aksel and myself, this young person was able to open her heart and share more about the origin of her pain and the extent of her suffering. Essentially, Aksel and I quietly held the space for Jana, listening with compassion, understanding, and empathy.

School protocol dictated that disclosure of a suicide attempt required that Jana be transported by a police officer to the nearby hospital for further assessment. The thought of riding in the police car created intense anxiety for her, based upon past negative experiences with police visiting her home. Thus, I rode in the squad car and a staff member from school drove my SUV with Aksel in the back. I called ahead and received permission from the head nurse to bring Aksel into the ER.

When we arrived at the hospital, Aksel and I entered the ER area. Interestingly, nurses and doctors began coming up to us wanting to pet Aksel. Some even took out their cell phones and captured selfies with Aksel! To say this was a welcome distraction from the otherwise heaviness of the situation was an understatement. His presence seemed to lift the spirits of all those nearby.

Jana was placed in a room and the three of us sat and waited for a doctor to assess her. Aksel's beautiful, calm presence seemed to ease Jana's anxiety, fear, and uncertainty. Once the doctor met with her, Jana was placed on a 72-hour hold in a psychiatric hospital. She went on to continue with animal-assisted counseling with myself, Aksel, and the horses at my private practice/ranch.

That was many years ago, so it came as a surprise when Jana contacted me 6 years later. She shared the impact Aksel, the horses, and I had in her life and asked to begin counseling again. It is so rewarding to see this young woman now choosing to face her challenges by addressing them head on instead of running away or considering suicide. Her healing journey continues, one I believe was initiated by Aksel.

Aksel passed away in 2019 at the age of 8 but he made a positive impact in the lives of so many. Rest in peace, buddy Aksel, and thank you for the difference you made in the lives of Jana and many others.

Discussion Questions:

1   What traits might animals like Aksel have that allow for this openness to occur?
2   What insight or lessons have you gained because of interaction with animals in your own life?
3   What types of animals do you feel are best suited for offering emotional support to people?

43 A Gentle Giant and an Anxious Teen

Jane Jenkins

Throughout my undergrad and graduate programs as a non-traditional student, I wrote about what I thought was the positive impact of horses on humans. I drew much of my knowledge from personal experience and from my very special relationship with a cranky little sorrel quarter horse that assisted me through a lot of my own adolescent angst. Now, here I was; a green-around-the-gills master's level mental health clinician providing therapeutic services with the opportunity to test this positive impact for real.

I had been assigned to provide in-home services for a teenage girl who had chronic and frequent school refusal. Sometimes she went to school once or twice per week, and sometimes she went to school once in two weeks. She used every strategy she could think of to avoid going to school. She was very smart and could easily catch up on the work, but she was slowly digging a hole she wouldn't be able to recover from as high school became more difficult and the workload much heavier. At the same time, I had a friend not far from her home who had a very large horse, a Belgian draft horse to be exact, who had suffered a leg injury and was on paddock rest.

I met with my teen client for our initial few sessions and I sensed there was more to the story than her not wanting to go to school. She told me about several incidents of misunderstandings with various friends and declared she was a "one and done" kind of girl. That is, if she had one difficulty with a friend, she ended the friendship. She was a little awkward socially, a bit sensitive, and navigating friendships had become too hard. But, now what? My clinical books did not prepare me for this! I decided to slow things down and just chat with her. I learned that she really liked animals, particularly big animals, like horses. I mentioned that I was a "horse person" and she became very interested in learning about them.

DOI: 10.4324/9781003204534-48

I wanted her to go to school and she wanted to learn about horses. So we made a deal. For every week that she attended school for at least four days, I would teach her about horses and take her to hang out with one. Was it a bribe? Possibly. Did it work perfectly? Nope. Did we both learn a lot thanks to a big, gentle Belgian horse? Definitely! The first four weeks she averaged four to five days of school per week. I was thinking to myself, "This is going great!" Then her attendance dipped after the two-week holiday break from school. She began averaging two days per week and this sustained for the next eight weeks. That was when our real work began.

She began to fall back to old behaviors, avoiding school and finding excuses to rationalize her behavior. While I continued to teach her about horses at the end of our sessions, we were not spending time with the horse. That was the deal. She began to really miss her horse time with the Belgian. One particular week, she reached a crossroads. She had one more day to reach her fourth day of attending school in order to see the horse. The pull of avoidance was strong. She called to tell me she did not feel well, and could we PLEASE go see the horse even if she missed school. After all, she felt "sick." I calmly empathized with her dilemma yet held to our agreement. I explained that in this moment she had a hard decision to make that really had little to do with me and everything to do with how strong she could be in order to push through the challenges to get herself to school and earn her horse time.

It was as if a light turned on. Somehow, she broke through her anxiety, got herself to school, and when I picked her up from school to go see the horse, she exhibited a sense of confidence and excitement I had not seen previously. She never looked back, attending school four to five days every week until our time together ended at the close of the school year. The horse had won her over and the motivation to maintain the bond with the horse overpowered her urge to continue giving in to avoidance.

The unexpected gains that followed were incredible. She began to express increased confidence as weeks of regularly attending school accumulated. She actually said, "I think I really LIKE school!" The goal of increasing her school attendance was met, but she began to gain other important skills from our giant, equine friend. She learned about his body language and began to identify her own affect based on watching his. With his body language as a mirror, she learned to use breathing techniques and mindfulness exercises (i.e. grooming, petting with intention) to help him relax, regulating herself at the same time.

Her ability to recognize and question unhelpful thoughts also increased exponentially. Originally, when the horse would move away from her to eat from the hay pile, she would assume he was annoyed with her, that she had brushed him incorrectly, or she had done something wrong. With practice, she was able to ask herself what else it could be. The phrase, "sometimes it's not about you, it's just about hay" became a joke between us. The icing on the cake was when she explained that her experiences with the horse had helped her repair a relationship at school. She had generalized what she had learned with the horse to her friendships outside the therapeutic setting.

What I saw unfold with this client impacted me forever. She validated what I knew to be true and what led to my current career path. I am so grateful to that gentle giant for making such an impact on my client. I think of him fondly and wish I could tell him how he changed a young girl's life… as well as mine.

Discussion Questions:

1   What "horse factors" do you think helped change the girl's behavior?
2   What mental health strategies might you integrate into a similar scenario to help a client succeed?

44 Therapy Dogs Help Adoption Succeed

Gary P. Cournoyer

I am a clinical social worker in private practice with my two therapy dogs, Iko, a fourteen-year-old Labrador mix, and Hooper, a seven-year-old beagle. Both are rescue dogs who have found their calling in helping children and families in crisis. We have had the experience of helping numerous children who had experienced many different types of trauma. A few years ago, a six-year-old girl, Annie, was referred to my office because she was acting out at her current placement, being physically and verbally aggressive to both peers and staff. Annie had a sad, abusive history, having been removed from her biological mother due to abuse and neglect.

During our first session, Annie wanted little to do with me, but she was enamored with my therapy dogs. She laid with the dogs and petted them throughout the session. I hoped that her connection with the dogs would eventually help me form a helpful, healing relationship with her. After a few sessions, I was asked to also start seeing her four-year-old sister, Bethany, who was also struggling with behavior problems. From the first session, Bethany also loved my therapy dogs and spent the sessions petting them while we talked.

One day, Annie confided in me that she had been told to never talk about family secrets outside the home. She said that this would be snitching and no one (not even police) can be trusted. Yet, after months of talking to me and petting Iko and Hooper, Annie and Bethany began to open up to me. In one pivotal session, Annie started to talk about the terrible experiences she had at her parents' home. Bethany started to yell at her that she is not supposed to talk about any of that with anybody. We spent the rest of the session talking about why secrets in families are usually not good.

During the next session with Iko's head in her lap, Annie continued talking and opened up about the physical and sexual abuse she suffered at home. Eventually, Bethany supported these statements. Based on

DOI: 10.4324/9781003204534-49

these conversations, visits with their family were suspended and eventually Annie and Bethany were freed for adoption. This entire process took approximately two years, throughout which they became closely bonded to Iko and Hooper. As our work together continued, the sisters were able to start to think of what they would like in a new family. What they requested from a new home brought tears to my eyes. They wanted parents who would not hurt them. They didn't want to be hungry all the time anymore. They wanted someone to tuck them in at night. And, they wanted a dog.

As I was reviewing homes to narrow down potential families, I kept their requests in mind and, eventually, was able to select a family. When this single woman, who would become their forever mom, came to my office to meet Annie and Bethany, she found them both sitting on the floor with Iko laying between them. The girls were delighted to find out that this woman had her own dog. The meeting went well, and more visits were scheduled. Happily, Annie and Bethany were placed with this mother and soon afterward, they were adopted. Because this mother lived in another state, we had to say goodbye. The farewell meetings in my office were bittersweet. Through tears of sadness and joy, they left Iko and Hooper (and me) for their new forever home. In my heart, I have no doubt that the credit for these girls' successful adoption lies with Iko and Hooper. These dogs were the conduit for these little girls learning to trust and love again. The last update I received about Annie and Bethany indicated that both sisters were doing well – and included an enclosed picture of two little smiling girls playing with their family dog.

Discussion Questions:

1   Why do you think it is so difficult for trauma survivors to connect with a therapist?
2   How do the therapy dogs help in the development of this therapeutic relationship?

45 Leo Awakens to the World

Shira Smilovici

Leo and his mother arrived at the doctor's office; at which time she received the news she dreaded: her son was diagnosed as falling within the Autistic Spectrum. She thought this was what she was going to hear since Leo was not interested in the world that surrounded him. He showed no motivation to share with his peers and avoided physical touch and eye contact; instead, he enjoyed being alone.

His mother, searching for the best treatment for Leo, found me and Siggi. Since the first moments together, Leo, Siggi, and I had a special connection. Although Leo didn't communicate like most people do, he could always find a way to let others know what he needed, even at 2.5 years of age (the age we first started working together). He seemed pretty peaceful in his inner world, smiling and playing; the problems started when he realized that he was part of a bigger world filled with other people that surrounded and affected him. He could only tolerate being held by his mother and, after time, me.

When we first started working together, he came twice a week to play with me and Siggi (my oldest therapy dog). Although he wouldn't go approach her, he'd allow for her to come near him. Gradually he began to allow closer contact. In fact, he began to get excited as she'd get closer. Some great moments were when she'd lick him; he'd start laughing, so I'd translate for him, saying how this felt like tickles, and he was enjoying it. After several times he started to verbalize his feelings on his own. Imagine how we all felt when he gave her his first kiss – this was the first time Leo had ever kissed a living being. This moment transformed his relationship with Siggi in one of his most significant relationships. During this time, he would come to every session, always looking forward to playing with her, cuddling, and even napping with her. Time with Siggi and I became his safe space where he was allowed to be himself, no pressure, where he was allowed to express what he wanted, when he wanted – a space of unconditional love.

DOI: 10.4324/9781003204534-50

Having such a safe environment gave him the security he needed to meet the world. He started noticing others around him, was able to show more empathy, watching his step (at first to not step on Siggi, then to not step on or kick others). When he'd accidentally step on Siggi, he'd apologize by petting and kissing her, his way of making everything better again. I would constantly interpret Siggi's body language for him, helping him realize how safe and comfortable she felt as she laid easily by his side.

The bond built between Leo and Siggi worked as a bridge between Leo and the world. He began to replicate what he learned with her to the world, starting with me. He created a strong bond with me, including me in his play time. Since then, he requested I joined the game he created with Siggi, this opened the opportunity for others to join him socially.

After a couple of years, Kika (also a therapy dog) came into the scene and automatically they bonded. His mother told me that Leo would ask about the girls before he went to sleep every night. Leo developed a non-verbal language with the girls that helped him communicate with the world, allowing him to express his feelings, and feel supported, loved, and accepted. Their relationship lasted a little over 5 years and was such a successful experience for all of us who were part of his treatment. This relationship changed all of us for the better and has always remained one of my favorite memories.

Discussion Questions:

1 How do you feel a bond with a dog can be used as a model with people for those with autism?
2 Do you feel there are benefits unique to dogs that are not present with other types of animals for people with autism?

Part 6
Adults

46 Jaeger's Gifts

Shannan Anderson

I have always had a fear of German Shepherds. Maybe it's their large size, dark piercing eyes, loud threatening bark, or sharp teeth – or a combination of it all! To my surprise though, Jaeger, a very confident and obedient German Shepherd, became one of my favorite therapy dogs at my job as a Recreation Therapist at a VA Hospital. His ability to connect to our Veterans was almost like magic. His confidence was infectious and his victory lap around the room after a job well done was fun.

I remember how Jaeger would watch the bottom of the door of my clinic treatment space, waiting for it to crack open. He would lay his head on the cool tile floor and watch the feet of people pass by on the other side of the door. His ears would turn toward any sound and, often, would turn only one ear toward the sound while keeping the other on the patient in the room to show how good he was at multitasking. This gift he gave our Veterans was the gift of, "Don't worry, I got your back".

It's a well-known fact that Veterans are trained to stick together. No one is left behind and we work together to complete the mission. For Veterans working through trauma, this is a very welcomed gift.

Trauma can hit us out of nowhere. It is defined by each one of us differently. Sometimes it's physical in nature and sometimes emotional, but often it is both. No matter the reason or the cause, I regularly see people at their worst. I often see adults struggling with relearning to walk and talk again after sustaining an injury to their head due to a fall, a freak car accident, or a stroke.

Bob became my patient on our rehabilitation unit following his stroke. Bob was a short man with little to no hair who sat in his wheelchair looking lost when I first met him. His stroke affected his ability to speak and swallow. I formulated all my questions so he could respond

DOI: 10.4324/9781003204534-52

with a yes or no when I completed my initial assessment and identified his leisure interests. I even wrote out words as it seemed to help his comprehension. I explained my role as a Recreation Therapist on the rehabilitation unit and he sat staring blankly, unsure of how I could help him through the trauma of his stroke.

Later, I connected with his wife and learned the 75-year-old Army Veteran had a pet dog at home whom he cherished deeply and had a passion for cooking. These are important details for me as a Recreation Therapist as I often find ways to incorporate their leisure interests into their personal goals and our therapy sessions.

After reviewing his medical chart and connecting with his Speech Therapist, I determined he wouldn't be eating anything he cooked anytime soon due to his puréed and thickened liquid diet. Disappointed though determined, I sat back in my office pondering how I could help this man until it came to me. This idea, unbeknownst to me at the time, would end up helping him heal and return home to his wife and his pet dog.

I contacted my therapy dog volunteer about my idea and we set a date for her and her therapy dog, Jaeger, to visit. I talked to Bob about what I had planned and he was delighted. Combining his interests, I asked if he could make homemade dog treats for Jaeger. Imagine the smiles and pride that beamed from his face as he handed the peanut butter treat in the shape of a dog bone to an eager and willing therapy dog. Bob was delighted – he had a purpose. He had something of meaning back in his life. He could do something he once enjoyed and learned he could enjoy again.

What better gift could a person receive in a time of turmoil and tragedy than the realization that they can still contribute. That all is not lost. In this case, it was realizing that he could still cook and bond with a dog, and eventually, his own dog again. Jaeger had done his magic. While Bob did not regain his ability to verbally communicate, he did regain the ability to tap into the bond he had with his own dog long before the stroke ever occurred – thanks to Jaeger.

I am happy to report not only do I see people at their worst, I see them at their best too. I see people reach inside themselves and find untapped resources. I have witnessed countless times that dogs like Jaeger help facilitate this process. I truly believe animals can work magic and help us heal.

Discussion Questions:

1 What gifts have you received from a current or former pet?
2 How could or how has a pet helped you through a difficult situation in your life?
3 How could your dog help someone else?

47 The Whirlwind That Changed My Life…

Úrsula Aragunde-Kohl

Sometimes, the most unexpected things change the core fabric of who you are and who you become. Even something as simple as seeing a dog through a window at a pet shop can turn your world on its head and completely shift your outlook.

For me, this life-altering event occurred when I met my first therapy dog, Nina. She came to me as an unwanted accident. Nina was a black and white Border Collie mix with a rowdy temperament. She was also the first dog I had ever worked with and trained. Looking back now, I realize that a dog like Nina probably wasn't the best choice for a first-time dog guardian like myself. Nina was so poorly socialized she didn't even know how to climb stairs.

Most dog trainers will tell you not to get a Border Collie because they require significant amounts of structured training and exercise to keep them in line. Without it, they can become a real challenge. To be candid with you, I'm delighted I didn't know that at the time. I don't think it would have stopped me from choosing her (which, in reality, I didn't; she really didn't give me much choice with the famous look collies can provide), and that would have been the worst mistake of my life because she became my very best friend.

It didn't take long after getting Nina for me to realize that she needed a great deal of attention, stimulation, and strict training. She was rowdy from the get-go, constantly bouncing around like a ball. She also had a strange fear of children, likely from being cramped up for weeks on end in a cage with children poking their hands through her cell. Because of these traits, though, she and I trained together for a long time—she to be a (good) therapy dog and I as a clinical psychologist. When we had both graduated from our respective programs (I with a Doctorate and she with an official therapy dog certificate), we realized we needed a new mission.

DOI: 10.4324/9781003204534-53

In time, we began to visit homes for the elderly every week. The residents loved her, and many would share stories about the dogs they had, had lost, or were forced to give up because they had to relocate to a residential living environment. Nina loved being there just as much as they loved having her, and many of the residents would keep treats on hand just for her.

One day, while visiting one of our usual nursing homes, an experience changed my life.

When we walked in, I was told about a man who had heard about Nina and wanted to see her. We hadn't interacted with him yet because he had severe Parkinson's and was confined to his room most of the time. What we weren't told, however, was just how intense it was. A nurse led Nina and me down a hallway, where we stopped just outside a door.

We walked into the room, and I could immediately see what the staff had been talking about. The man was lying down, and his involuntary movements were so bad, they were shaking his whole bed. The shaking sound would bounce off the walls and make it difficult to have a conversation. A nurse had to accompany us and help him sit up.

Yet, he smiled from ear to ear the moment he saw Nina. We all watched in awe as the man's shakes gradually petered out, and he was able to interact with Nina. He started petting her very gently with only the slightest bit of trembling. It was like night and day from the man we had seen only moments before when we walked in.

That experience marked me for life. It's essentially one of the main reasons I knew I needed to pursue the human-animal bond as a career path. Sometime after that happened, I also started a nonprofit dedicated to rescuing cats and dogs here in Puerto Rico. The charity's mission is to educate the Puerto Rican community about compassion, kindness, and responsible guardianship. Nina became our organization's first spokesdog and therapy dog, visiting schools, universities, and organizations all over the island.

During her tenure, she positively impacted countless children, teenagers, and adults. Nina has since passed away, but her spirit lives on as a beacon of light within our organization. Everyone who worked with Nina loved her, including myself and the thousands of hands who petted her when we visited. I do not doubt that I will continue to work with other therapy dogs; however, I doubt many will be quite as wily and rowdy as Nina was. I still miss her every day. Rest easy, Nina. You may be gone, but you will never be forgotten.

Discussion Questions:

1   What are the possible consequences of choosing a highly intelligent and active dog as a therapy dog in terms of training, well-being, and needs of the animal?
2   What are the considerations we must have in working with older adults in animal-assisted interventions?

48 My Therapy Dogs Saved My Life

Megan C.W. Bridges

My name is Megan and I served as the coordinator for the Calhoun County Family Drug Court, a specialty treatment court in Calhoun County, Alabama, from 2016 to 2021. From my first days, I incorporated animal-assisted activities and eventually animal-assisted interventions within the specialty treatment court. It was incredible to see the change in participants' attitudes when they encountered my therapy dogs.

My chosen co-therapists during my employment at Calhoun County Family Drug Court were canines who live with me and my husband. I have three pups who would take turns accompanying me to work on a daily basis. The first one is a stray pup who came to me through a neighbor. His name is Squiggle and he is a vocal, outgoing, food snatching Mountain Feist/Dachshund mix. The second is a pure Papillion named Whisper, who quietly judges people before approaching, whimpering, and asking for a lap to sit in. And finally, my third pup, who is also a Papillion, although he is three times the size of a normal Papillion! His name is Ringo and his personality is larger than life. He adores everyone he meets and wants to join in any activity suggested. He is also my dog who seems most gifted at communicating in the dog's native language. Ringo is exceptional at meeting and getting along with unfamiliar dogs and can diffuse an overactive or agitated dog's behavior with a flick of his tail and a blink of his eye. All skills I'm envious of and learn from daily.

When I agreed to write my contribution for this text, I planned to tell you how one of my amazing canine partners helped to change the life of one of my incredible Family Drug Court participants; however, I am writing a different story; my story. My personal story is enough to fill several books, but I will suffice by saying that while 2020 was a difficult year for many people, it struck me personally by triggering a major episode of depression, anxiety, and PTSD (post-traumatic stress disorder) that lasted well into 2021.

DOI: 10.4324/9781003204534-54

Through my deepening depression, I and my canine cohorts were able to continue to lead my specialty treatment court, serving our community, and in the process earned the Alabama Association of Drug Court Specialists' annual Chief Justice Sue Bell Cobb Appreciation Award for being the most outstanding treatment court in the State of Alabama. Unfortunately, almost immediately after receiving the award, I was told my services were no longer needed. Of course, the loss of such a meaningful position was a huge blow, especially in my depressed state, and I did the unthinkable – I considered suicide!

The thing about mental health issues and suicidal ideations is that they don't discriminate. It did not matter that I had developed a State recognized treatment court in less than five years, that I had two Master's degrees, a beautiful marriage, and had been asked to speak at multiple national and local professional conferences on my favorite topic – animal-assisted therapy. None of those things could keep me from wanting to leave it all behind and permanently remove myself from the pain and anger I was experiencing.

Luckily, I have the most intuitive, naturally skilled "therapy dogs". It is not an overstatement to say that my boys saved my life. They gave me purpose when I had trouble finding my own. Looking into Whisper's eyes inspired me. It helped me take the steps necessary to get help, to find strength, and to heal. Ringo's personality kept me up and moving, getting me outside, and motivating me to exercise. And Squiggle's unending love kept me determined to keep moving forward, to continue searching for my purpose, my reason to live.

At the time of this writing, I am currently employed, doing what I do best – loving and helping those who abuse substances and heal from their wounds and traumas. I, myself, am in therapy, also healing my wounds and traumas. And my dogs are living their best life with my retired husband who stays at home and responds to their every beck and call. It has taken us some time, but I am on the mend and moving in the right direction. I have relocated my purpose, my career as an animal-assisted therapist is not over, and my dogs are on a much-deserved sabbatical.

In the process, I have learned what I have known all along – everything happens for a reason and I have been placed on this earth to do what my dogs do naturally, and that is to love those around me, especially those who are suffering the most, even if that person is myself.

Discussion Questions:

1   In what ways do you think my mental status impacted my therapy
dogs' emotional and physical well-being?
2   Do you think the abrupt change in the dogs' "work schedule"
affected their quality of life? If so, how?
3   What precautions can be put in place to ensure the mental and
physical health of therapy animals?

49 Miss Emmie
A Big "Braveheart" in a Tiny Package

Donna Clarke

I have had the great joy of being able to work with an amazing partner over the years. She has boundless empathy, presence, and humor, as well as the unique ability to join with clients in ways unimaginable. Ever giving, ever trying. Always with care. This is her story.

"All set for work?" I ask, and eagerly, she runs in.

A tiny 5.5 pound Teacup Poodle with the heart of a giant. Tail wagging, ready to go, Miss Emmie caringly worked with me as my clients shared their life stories of joy, pain, triumph, tragedy, and sorrow. During sessions, she shared a perfectly timed sigh, snuggle, or gaze, and clients responded, opening up, feeling safe, and expressing their thoughts, feelings, and perceptions, through … and with … little Miss Emmie. Clients came to look forward to sharing their journeys with her. Often they would ask in advance if she would be joining the session. One client, journeying through her own exploration of self-care after grief and loss, came to a personal insight as we were scheduling for our next session. She had wanted to schedule her next appointment with Miss Emmy present; however, she did not have availability during Emmie's hours the following week. We explored this conundrum from the shared perspective of self-care.

"Miss Emmie would love to spend time with you next week, and she also needs her self-care between clients," I shared, "What do you think she would want to do?"

"Miss Emmie would want to say 'Yes,' and she needs to say 'No.' She needs good boundaries." The client replied, "I could use some of those, too! Let's try another day."

Miss Emmie and I worked well together, providing comfort to our clients, as they processed their journeys. And then came COVID.

The world seemed to shift. With lockdowns, sessions moved to Telemental Health, and Miss Emmie and I found ourselves shifting right along with it. As a Board Certified Telemental Health Provider,

DOI: 10.4324/9781003204534-55

I knew I would find a path. But what of Miss Emmie? She's my partner ... we knew we would find a way. We simply had to.

"All set for work?" I asked. Again, Miss Emmie came running, seemingly to signal she was ready for a new adventure. Sitting next to me on her own special chair, enabling her to join me in the session, as she wishes, we began.

One day, while working with a client, "Mary," Miss Emmie was especially attentive, gazing inquisitively at the computer monitor, sitting straight and tall, her very big heart ever present.

"I feel like a failure. Why can't I get it right?" the client shared. Mary looked at Miss Emmie.

"Why can't I be brave like Miss Emmie?" She asked.

Emmie looked at the screen, then, as if awaiting my response, she looked at me.

"What do you think Emmie is thinking about this?" I asked Mary.

"She is so strong and brave. I wish I could be as brave as she is," the client said. Emmie sits and listens, looking at the screen as I pet her.

"What do you think gives her strength?" I ask.

Mary thought for a moment and shared "people who love her."

We sit a moment to ponder. "I have people who love me, too," the client continued. "Just like Emmie, but I don't like to ask for help."

We process and examine how it might have been that Emmie would ask for help as such a small dog.

Weeks later, Emmie is standing, wagging her tail on my desk in front of the screen while Mary is saying "Hello."

"She is always so glad to see me, my little Braveheart!" Mary observed.

Emmie sits and begins to listen intently while the client starts to share. "What makes Emmie so strong?" she queried again.

"That's a great question. What do you think it might be?" I responded.

"She gets up every day and takes it on." The client shared, "She is a little Braveheart!"

We explore how it might be that Emmie can take on each day with such gusto. We explore presence, attunement, and process. Weeks pass and Emmie listens as the client shares.

While she is talking, the client observes Miss Emmie and says, "Miss Emmie looks sad, do you think she is sad for me?"

"What do you think she would say to you?" I asked.

"She would tell me it is OK to be sad because she has sad days, too" Mary responded. We processed and discussed tools and strategies both the client and Miss Emmie might utilize when feeling sad.

A few weeks later, while processing Mary's use of tools related to a triggering event, she shared,

"Do you know what?"

"What?" I asked.

"I can be as strong as Emmie, the Braveheart. After all, if she is so small and can have a Braveheart, I can have a Braveheart too."

And so, we continue on our journey, Miss Emmie and I. I am so ever thankful to have a partner whose eyes provide warmth and understanding, and who can receive the stories of countless clients with empathy and presence, allowing them to feel heard and felt, even while working through a screen.

Discussion Questions:

1   What are some tools and strategies one might utilize to foster a connection utilizing Telemental Health with a canine co-therapist?

2   What are some ways a therapist might utilize a client's bond with their own dog to foster connections and increase presence and attunement?

3   What do you perceive "Mary's" self-narrative might be and what tools were utilized to shift her narrative?

50 Being and Becoming

The Transformative Power and Resilience of Person-Canine Bonds

Cassandra Hanrahan

Ramón – Being IN the Moment

I met Ramón in a parking lot. He sprang out of the car on the end of a very long leash, looping like a snake, his body striking in and out of view, the white patch on his chest flashing in the dusky November air. A person with whom I had worked was helping to re-home this dog. Not knowing anything about beagles, I agreed to meet. Ramón was my first dog; life with him was extraordinary.

I was fully responsible for him, unlike the one with whom I grew up. Walking with Ramón, our main event, was at first a strange experience. It was the 'strolling' that was unfamiliar to me. The 'being outside,' in motion, with no destination or itinerary, other than the walk itself. So, it was Ramón who keenly guided us along the neighborhood sidewalks and across fields. Stopping here and there, sniffing this and that, particularizing a world beyond my senses. Eventually, our daily walks became habitual, but rarely routine. On one memorable occasion, a stillness and quiet bore a hole in space and slowed time within the grey observant air; it was as though we were the only two in the world. Ramón had stopped in front of a bush and although at first it seemed to be a regular stop, it became a meditation that enveloped us. He sniffed along the length of a branch, singled out from the many. Slowly and deliberately, beginning at the center moving outward to the very tip, pausing at intervals. Inhale. Exhale. As I watched him do this, time and place became diluted leaving relation and being my only points of reference. There was Ramón (al) One, the branch, and me (al)One. Afterwards, realizing how I had been utterly absorbed into that moment, in Ramón's study, or mine of him, I appreciated our walks even more. In them I put my faith – a daily deliverance.

DOI: 10.4324/9781003204534-56

Aureole – Becoming THE Moment

I met Aureole one early autumn morning in cottage country. I had noticed him watching me from a safe distance among the trees while I took a rather cool swim. From the lake, I watched him back and though initially I wasn't quite sure what it was, I saw something was not quite right. As I got out of the water, his eyes followed me. When I walked toward him, he shuffled, unable to stand, he crouched. I saw as I neared, he was emaciated, scared, likely injured, and (al)One. Lost or abandoned I didn't know, but after visiting a local vet and some inquiries, Aureole came home to the city to be fostered. I'll never forget our night drive into downtown Toronto. I think it was Aureole's first time in a car, seeing the skyscrapers and bright lights of zooming vehicles. I imagine it must have felt like skyrocketing into outer space.

Once acclimatized to city life, Aureole introduced me to alleys and park benches that until his arrival had been props in the wonted backdrop of my quotidian life. In a short time, I adopted Aureole, my second dog; life with him was extraordinary. I'll never forget one summer day, saturated with heat, I went to a park to cool off in the shade of the trees and grass, away from the concrete. Arrival under the park's canopy was like diving into water. Aureole bowed and ran; I stretched out onto the cool ground. Against muffled traffic noise, I heard a rhythmic reverberation coming up through the ground. It sounded like the pounding hoofs of wild horses. It couldn't be and in that equanimous moment I lifted my head and saw Aureole galloping – and saw transcendence. Aureole's wavy black and white hair blowing against swirls of turquoise and green and earth – he and I (al)One in reverence.

Patrick – Being WITH the Moment

Patrick, a one-year-old shy and energetic husky shepherd, was supposed to be a ten-year-old female beagle named Rosie. What I mean is, when I arrived at the shelter to visit and hopefully adopt Rosie, she was gone; whom I met instead was Patrick. Patrick was a dog with nervous eyes, a smile that reached from ear to ear, and folded ears that looked as though they were dipped in chocolate. After a walk and some reassuring conversation, Patrick seemed happy to ride home in my car, perched on the back seat, intently surveying the passing scenery, his face lit. He became my third dog; life with him was extraordinary. Although keen and curious, Patrick was also apprehensive and reacted at times with fear-based aggression. He responded to kindness and love and was acutely attentive. He needed to know what was right, not only what was wrong.

He gifted me his trust to navigate society, the world around him. And as I did – he accompanied me wholly and unconditionally. In our house, he abided my every word, which I chose carefully, praising silence and communal efforts so that he could relax and stand down. Patrick learned, too, to choose his sounds carefully. Loyal and steadfast, Patrick had a tremendous ability to be with and present – he taught me the splendor of shared tranquility. In the more-than-human world, on walks, we navigated together. On one particular outing on a wooded winter trail at dawn, the world insulated in the mild morning and deep snow, Patrick stood placid against the white and orange sky among sleeping trees off trail – (al)One in resonance with what there was in the moment – the opulence of season, the weather, our companionship.

Each of these personal experiences has shaped my life and worldview. They illustrate the essence and power of the human-animal bond and explain the scaffolding for my teaching and research around the inclusion of human-animal interaction and AAI work.

Discussion Questions:

1 Thinking about these three reflections, as well as your own memories, what are some key behaviors and attributes (e.g., kindness) of positive human-animal interactions, and relational bonds more specifically, that inform mutual growth and resilience?

2 Benefits from human-animal relations or zooeyia are central to animal-assisted interventions, but human-animal bonds per se are not always present in animal-assisted interventions. When working with clients who have little or no experience with companion animals, and/or who still hold outdated views about animals, what can practitioners do to inspire clients to be open and receptive, and to ultimately awaken attitudinal changes toward other animals?

3 The relational bonds that emerge out of individuals' lived experiences testify to the ways such companionable relations are dynamic, albeit informal interventions. Thinking about your own experiences, in life and/or in your practice, in what ways might the field of animal-assisted interventions be extended to provide leadership on healthy human-animal interactions more generally, with the aim of fostering more globally sustainable communities?

51 Pinella's Purpose

Tiana Kelly

Eyes as big as buttons amid a sea of black, velvety fur. A cold, wet nose. Seven tiny puppies all born with hearts to serve and paws preparing to walk their life-changing missions. The tiniest of the litter, Pinella's story began on September 21, 2015 at Susquehanna Service Dogs. As a new service-dog-in-training, she navigated her first few weeks of life much like that of a college student. Much like that of the student whose life she would one day change.

There was so much to explore. To Pinella, her world was filled with intriguing sights and sounds, desirous smells, and people she learned to trust and rely upon. Not yet known was that she was not alone in this journey of adjustments. As Pinella's formative weeks of training were underway, a young woman had just begun her first years as a student at a nearby college. It would not be long before one day their paths would cross in a life-saving encounter.

Attending college can be a magical experience. There is the chance to develop ever-lasting friendships, create life-enriching memories, and ignite a passion for your life's work. Less talked about is the complicated nature of adjusting to life as a college student.

Self-confidence wavers. Feelings of anxiety and depression emerge like peaks and valleys across a mountainous landscape. In a sea of changes, there is a longing for predictability and certainty. The desire for connection is burning, but the urge to avoid it is stronger. There are supportive resources right at your fingertips, yet they feel a galaxy away. It feels like you are all alone, with little anybody can do to make things better. That is, until a black Labrador service-dog-in-training named Pinella enters your life.

Pinella's journey as my service-dog-in-training was short-lived but monumental. The first-ever service dog to be raised on the campus, she pranced the residence halls with a confident stature and puppy eyes that melted the hearts of every resident she met. With me as her puppy

DOI: 10.4324/9781003204534-57

raiser, she learned basic service dog cues with the intention to someday help someone live a more independent life. Behind the scenes, however, she was shaping the emotional health of those who needed her most.

One night, I was startled with the sound of an abrupt, sharp, and demanding knock on my door. As the floor's resident assistant (who also happened to have a six-month-old puppy), this was not an unfamiliar sound to me. However, the urgency behind this particular knock was unsettling. Pinella in tow, I answered the door without an ounce of foresight into the night that was about to unfold.

There stood a concerned roommate, sobbing uncontrollably but brave enough to know she needed help. It took powerful concentration to decipher the broken words trying to escape between her steady tears. "Locked in the bathroom." "Hurt." "Doesn't want to live." I heard enough. I called for help and rushed to the student in need. Little did I know, the most powerful therapeutic tool remained on the other side of my door: Pinella.

I arrived to witness a student in distress. I used my training, dug deep into my bank of empathy skills, validated her emotions, and encouraged her to accept help. It was clear to me that her pain ran deep and, as is common for so many who have lost the will to live, I imagine hope was nothing but a shattered illusion for her. Yet, her strength emanated. On her own accord, she identified the one source of hope she had that night: Pinella. "I just want to see Pinella." As clear as a cloudless day, she spoke those words to me. I stood for a brief moment, collecting my thoughts and questioning how someone in such distress could so clearly articulate what it was that she needed.

It should come as no surprise that her life-saving tool was the tiny, clumsy but confident, four-legged companion who sat waiting behind my door for her moment to shine. *That* is the human-animal bond. I ran down to my room and told this bundle of hope about the very important job I had for her. Yet, many anxious thoughts swirled through my mind. "She's just a puppy. Can she handle this?" "What if she pees everywhere or barks or jumps around like a six-month-old, uncontrollable puppy?" Like a dog after an unwanted bath, I shook those thoughts out of my head and had to place unwavering trust in the human-animal bond.

We approached the student's door. Deep breaths. Without cue, Pinella took a quick assessment of the situation, walked calmly to the student in distress, and positioned herself right near the student's lap to be petted. I observed with wonder and felt an overwhelming sense of comfort and relief as I witnessed distress transform to peace, hopelessness shift to hopefulness, and tear-stricken faces illuminate happiness.

The power of the human-animal bond is unquestionable. Pinella ultimately had her own anxieties that prevented her from service dog work. However, as my very important pet, I continue to experience her therapeutic impact, and we now share this gift with others in our work as a therapy dog team. That is Pinella's purpose.

Discussion Questions:

1   Reflecting on your entire reading of this story, what emotions emerged for you?
2   How can animals be incorporated as sources of hope in our daily lives?

52 A Golden Tail of Inter-Generational Bonds

Patrick J. Kirnan and Jean P. Kirnan

Canes and walkers shuffled about the lobby, the local news broadcast lingered in the background, and down the hall, the commotion and excitement surrounding another bingo night could be heard. It was an "old folks' home", in every way, a community unto itself. Many of the residents had crossed into the land of forgotten elders. In this final chapter of life, relatives, and memories became a part of the past as visitations and a link to the outside world slowly disappeared. But for a time, the Stony Brook Assisted Living Home was given a bright, golden light. In the late 2000s, if you looked at the activity board, down at the bottom there was a new visitor, Nellie, a loving golden retriever and local therapy dog.

Spanning generations and species, the collection of individuals who participated in the visits was an eclectic bunch. There was of course, Nellie, the pup and star of the show. She arrived at Stony Brook Assisted Living with her credentials: a Therapy Dog International ID card. Pat, a teenage boy, was there to fulfill a community service requirement for school, accompanied by Jean, his mom, who was Nellie's official handler. Like most teens, he wasn't thrilled to give up an hour of his free time to a group of old strangers. Soon enough, however, the "onerous" task of community service evolved into positive experiences as the collective stresses dissipated, and a group who would otherwise never have known each other, shared their stories and bonded.

The warmth and oneness that came with the experience of bringing a dog into the residence were truly infectious emotions. Like the naïve innocence of youth, Nellie had no preconceived notion of what the old folks' home was. She didn't act any different when we walked into the memory impaired unit nor notice disfigurements, sensory loss, or mobility limitations. She was simply happy to just be – to share in whatever life was there. By proxy, all who shared the space with Nellie were

DOI: 10.4324/9781003204534-58

invited to also change their lens. Even if that change was limited to a few moments of petting her soft, warm coat, it was evident that this exchange of energy was unique.

You see, not everyone had a son or daughter to come visit and bring the grandkids. For some, this was all they had left; themselves and any company they could keep within the four walls of the assisted living home. The loneliness was palpable. To know that you're in the final chapter of life, and that no one is coming to knock on your door to just say hello. We questioned ourselves; how can we inject life to those who are at the end of theirs? While planned activities can feel staged, clinical, or even insincere – a dog remains genuine. They can enter a room, spread joy simply by wagging their tail, and inviting a head rub. A dog doesn't demand that you speak, nor does it ask you to listen, it merely reminds you that you are here, and that we are here together, and that not being alone is something worth wagging your tail about.

Like any new activity, the Monday nights with Nellie started small, but with word of mouth, we found ourselves with a slate of regulars. To the point where we had to make a bigger sitting circle, and quite literally make the rounds with Nellie to ensure everyone got face time. While the seniors had a lot in common and reason to socialize, it's worth noting that several relationships were fostered, or further developed *specifically* because of Nellie's presence. For example, one resident, June, shared stories of the dog she had as a child and another resident, Pete, talked about the family beagle and the positive impact he had on his children. Almost everybody had their own "dog story" and whether it was a pup they owned or a memory of another, it was Nellie's presence that provided the invitation to share.

Over the years, our visits proved time and again that regardless of age, gender, mood, or disability, Nellie was a social lubricant that transcended demographics and generations. Everyone seemed to get something from the sense of community and the warmth in those room, and most powerfully for Pat, as an adolescent, it was the opportunity to witness this emotional exchange. At the age of 14, Pat learned a dog could make a lonely adult feel loved and heard once again. Better yet, he saw that community service was something that could be transformative and reciprocal, not merely a requirement to be checked off. Dogs have remained an instrumental part of his life and a source of unity within his family, having a significant positive impact on his mental health from adolescence into and throughout adulthood. In Pat's words, "Dogs have continued to provide a steady source of calm during life transitions, especially when my family has not been around".

Discussion Questions:

1 How does the story of Nellie represent the idea of an animal being a social lubricant?
2 Who are the parties in this dynamic and what "gifts" are being exchanged between them?
3 What are the potential benefits for youth of inter-generational service opportunities like the one described here?

53 You Are Here

Elizabeth Lynch

I absently fingered the button for number seven as I entered the elevator. My partner glided in and automatically sat in the corner of the elevator next to me. My mind was still occupied by the ramifications of a lecture that I listened to at the International Association of Human-Animal Interaction Organizations (IAHAIO) conference the previous week. The speaker's topic was the placebo effect, whereby a patient's symptoms could improve by up to 40% based on nothing but the belief in the power of a sugar pill.

The elevator doors slid open revealing the sunlight infused corridor of Stamford Hospital's cardiology unit. For the past three years, my partner Coconut and I had been visiting patients as a Pet Partners registered therapy animal team. Coconut was a 10-year-old mixed breed dog. A sleek, 65 pound, big, brown, hound; whom I found at the Yonkers, NY Animal Shelter at the age of three. He was often mistaken for a ridge-less Ridgeback, but his DNA test revealed him to be a Pitbull/Dalmatian/Lab mix.

I walked along, flanked by the white walls which were covered with beautiful artwork and photographs. I stopped at the first doorway. As I knocked and popped my head into the room, Coco dutifully sat and waited. I asked cheerfully, "Would you like a visit from a therapy dog?"

The middle-aged man was alone in the hospital room. The bed was made with crisp sheets, untouched. He stood in the middle of the space wearing a buttoned-down dress shirt, khakis, and loafers. His face held an occupied and closed expression which conveyed he was waiting for something, or perhaps wanted to be elsewhere. I assumed that he was waiting for a family member, who had been taken for a procedure somewhere in the hospital.

I asked again, "I have my therapy dog, Coconut, with me today. Would you like to see him?" I reassured the gentleman that it was OK for family members to visit and get some therapy too.

DOI: 10.4324/9781003204534-59

He softened his shoulders a bit, sighed, and stated that he really didn't need any therapy; but he would say hello to my dog.

Coco and I walked into the room, and I began chatting a bit about the weather. Coco stayed by my side. In order to cope with the slippery hospital floors, he sat with his hind legs splayed unevenly and used his tail as an additional anchor point. His face projected a calm, relaxed expression: wide open mouth, tongue lolling, and soft brown eyes; smiling at the man in front of us.

When the man confessed that he was there for a surgery, the conversation took an unexpected turn. Immediately, his expression changed, and there was a palpable tension in the room. The professed patient sat down heavily on the bed. Quietly, Coco slipped from my side and placed his body broadside against the man's knees and leaned in; his version of a hug. The patient chuckled softly and ruffled Coco's neck and stroked his ears.

As he fussed with Coco's fur, the man began to recite his medical history, the seriousness of his heart surgery, the possible complications, and the complexity of the procedure which he was facing. As if deep in a trance, he rhythmically stroked Coconut's smooth body from neck to shoulder to haunch, over and over. Methodically and as steady as a metronome, his hands fell on Coconut's body. As he reached the end of Coco's topline, his hands returned to Coconut's head. Each cupped hand landed with a soft plop, almost serving as a punctuation point for each of his concerns and worries. Finally, the man quieted his body and sat silently. After a moment, in a choked voice, he said, "I don't know what I will do if this procedure doesn't work."

In response to the man's anguish, Coco swiveled 90 degrees, squeezed between the man's knees, and pressed his upturned head and neck into the man's body. The patient smiled down at my dog and cleared his throat. Regaining his composure, he resumed his methodical stroking, this time stroking muzzle to head to neck to shoulders in a downward motion. Coconut's weight pressed firmly against the man's chest. The man proceeded to tell us how he had searched for the right surgeon and researched the right hospital. He discussed the pros and cons of the procedure. After several minutes, he took a very deep breath and blew out all the tension that he was holding in his body. He professed that he felt confident in the skill of his surgeons and had a feeling that everything would be OK.

The patient stood and thanked us for the visit. While walking us to the door, he urgently declared that he had to change. As he spoke, the fellow pointed to a hospital gown which I hadn't noticed, neatly folded at the head of the bed. He smiled as we left.

I have no idea whether the man's operation was a success. I do know that after getting some reassurance from a therapy animal, the gentleman was able to process his fears and find some peace. Perhaps Coconut helped him to gain confidence in his doctors. Maybe Coco helped to open the man's mind to the possibility of positive outcomes of the procedure. Maybe therapy animals are part of the placebo effect. If that is the case, I am confident that this fellow had a 40% increased chance of a positive surgical result.

Discussion Questions:

1   What interventions did Coconut deliver during his visit?
2   Do these interventions constitute an active treatment or a placebo? Does it matter?

54 *Humanimal* Connection in the Counseling Room

Where Lester the Dachshund Partner Weaves an Interspecies Bond

Emmanuelle Fournier Chouinard
Translated by Marie Tounissoux

"Wait for me, I'll be right back" says *My-Human*, turning to me. Her eyes and tone cue me to stay put. The door of the psychotherapy office closes. I lose sight of her and can feel the *bonding-cord that* binds us stretching. I'm not worried; I know what's next. She will soon come back with a human who will sit, seeking calmness from our contact, and leave. She'll then bring in another one, and another ... just another day at the office! Sniffing under the door, my nostrils fill with a peculiar mixture of fear and excitement. Blended with the scent of *My-Human*, I recognize the fragrance of the *cigarette-smoke-infused-frightened-Human*. He's a new one, met only once last week. I get excited ... *scratch, scratch* ... under the door. From my point of view, he's a strange human. Something's not quite right with him. I don't know how to explain. *My-Human* shared her theories with me (yes, she talks to me, pretending it helps her think). They are filled with picture-words such as *affiliative flow* that's clogged, *bonding-cord* that's poorly weaved, *barrier-bubble* turned *cocoon-shell* that cages and prevents connection ... Frankly speaking, all this is gibberish to me. However, I did detect injured animal signals from this strange human right from our first contact. Sometimes he is filled with pure rage and has an urge to attack (*My-Human*, for example). Other times, he is begging for help to escape his pain. Then, next thing you know, head down, he looks resigned and ready to die. Distress in others is upsetting; like a wave occasionally threatening to swallow me whole. Thankfully, *My-Human* and I are solidly bound by our *bonding-cord*, in addition to be firmly moored to the psychotherapeutic framework. In the face of our patients' great affective winds, we form a *Humanimal Team*.

DOI: 10.4324/9781003204534-60

I pity this particular human who has pretty much always been standing alone in a storm. *My-Human* thinks this has caused his heart, head, and body to become very ill. She says that within the *bonding-cord* that social animals weave together after birth (at times even in the womb) flows emotional nourishment as vital as the umbilical cord. But this human was barely fed. The little sustenance he got was meager, oftentimes even toxic. In survivor mode, his being only learned how to make voracious demands, all the while closing itself up and mistrustingly rejecting and spitting out any potential nourishment for fear of being poisoned. Working with *My-Human*, his unquenchable *thirst-for-others* intensifies. Upon our first contact last week, his helpless rage and despair worried me to the point where I didn't dare emerge from under my pile of blankets. Despite this, my drive to be there and engage was strong today, undeterred by *My-Human*'s desperate attempts to convince me otherwise. Something in that strange human is calling out to me. I therefore knew to fight for my right to choose. After all, the partner-animal's self-determination is a core principle of the *Humanimal Practice Model of Animal Mediation in Animal-Assisted Psychotherapy* developed by *My-Human*, isn't it?

The smell filling my nose bring me back to the now. Against a backdrop of footsteps, I hear the labored breathing of the *cigarette-smoke-infused-frightened-Human*. The door opens… Everyone takes a seat, the humans in armchairs and me on my pile of blankets. I sense *My-Human* slightly withdrawing, as if she is disengaging or holding back her *affiliative flow.* She does this with him, and also with me. Her affiliative flow barely trickles through our *bonding-cord*. I think the purpose is to avoid scaring or triggering him; to give him space. He is shaken anyway. And I am as well! You see, I was abandoned before my life with *My-Human* so I always feel unsettled when someone withdraws.

All of a sudden, I feel closer to this human. *My-Human* would say that his experience is echoing mine; past feelings surging into the present moment. The silence is stretching. Sensations invade it. Nature abhors a vacuum! *Pounding hearts, blood flowing in the ears, skin tingling intensely*… The affective wave hits me, both from inside and out. Who am I feeling? Him or me? I could get lost. I feel the human becoming rigid. Intolerable captivity. Unwilling to take it any longer, I seek support in *My-Human*'s eyes. Finding it, I yield to my eagerness to move. I roll over, rubbing my back on the floor.

"*You wiggle like a worm, Lester. All this is agitating you. Shhhhh… Caaalmmm… We'll find a way to settle together. Patience.*" The words whispered bring back a distant memory – *the relaxed panting of a mother dog. My mother?* I feel the human soften a hint. I lift my head up: that's when IT happens. *The human* and I both turn at the very same time. Our gaze meets and we see one another. I feel his hesitant *affiliative flow* brushing me. I want to respond. We are both thirsty for something the other can offer. I sense the change in him. He doesn't seem as scared; he feels safe with me, safe to risk bonding. Without breaking our gaze, I walk to him and timidly lay my paws on his knees.

Connection! I feel us both immersed in the warmth surging from within and from all around. We are both simultaneously the source and the vessel of this sensation and of this present moment. I feel my back prickling. Perhaps he also feels something, for in perfect sync, I turn around as he lifts his head: we are both looking at *My-Human* who bears a soft smile and watery eyes. "Ah! You meet at last... Lester, let me introduce you to Mr. Côté." The weaving of an interspecies bond, loaded with meaning, has begun: the *Humanimal Bond*.

In sweet memory of Lester, my dear Atomic-Sausage. For many, you were one of the Greats who knew not only how to show the way ... but also how to be a Voice!

Discussion Questions:

1   What characteristics make some dogs better therapy dogs?
2   How did *My-Human* ensure the welfare of Lester?
3   How did *My-Human* ensure Lester's active consent to participate? Why is the active consent of therapy dogs important?

Index

abused people: children, and dogs 135–6; children, and Forget Me Not Farm 17–19; college students, and dogs 64, 129; *see also* sexual abuse

adopted children and dogs 135–6

American Psychological Association (APA) 6

anxiety 66–8, 147–8; abused child and Forget Me Not Farm 18; child and teletherapy dog 114, 115; college students 156–8; dementia patients and dog 105; eating disorder and dogs 117; rabbit and campus pet therapy 40–1; suicidal student and dog 129–30

assisted living: dogs 144–5, 159–61; rabbits xxi–xxii, 39

autism spectrum disorder (ASD): dogs 32–3, 64, 120–2, 137–8; guinea pigs 43–5; horses 6–7

blindness: nursing home resident and rabbit xxi–xxii; sheep and at-risk children 23–4

bonds between people and dogs 153–5, 157–8

campus pet therapy, and rabbit 40–2

cancer patients, and dogs 92–3, 95–7

cardiology patient, and dog 162–4

Charlie's Acres 23–4

children: abused, and dogs 135–6; abused, and Forget Me Not Farm 17–19; adopted, and dogs

135–6; at-risk, and rescued farm animals 23–4; autism spectrum disorder, and dogs 32–3, 64, 120–2, 137–8; autistic spectrum disorder, and guinea pigs 43–5; autism spectrum disorder, and horses 6–7; communication differences, and dog 126–8; compassion, and dogs 123–5; confidence building, and guinea pigs 29–30; fetal alcohol syndrome, and dog/pigs 109–10; flood victim, and dog 61; hospital patient, and rabbit 46–8; incarcerated, and dog 83–5; mass shooting victims, and dogs 77–8, 102–3; school, and dog 111–12; sensory processing needs, and rabbits 38–9; teletherapy dogs 114–16; tornado victim, and dog 55–6

cognitively impaired youth, and dogs 98–100

colleges *see* universities and colleges

communication differences, and dog 126–8

compassion development through dogs 123–5

context, miniature donkey and memory care facility resident 20–2

court-ordered therapy and dogs 81–2

COVID-19 pandemic: dog ownership 95; school students 112; teletherapy dogs 90, 114–16, 150–2

cow, and abused child 17–18

dementia: and dog 104–6; and horse 15–16

depression, and dogs 147–8; college students 129, 156–8

dogs: abused student 64; adopted children 135–6; anxiety 147–8, 156–8; autistic spectrum disorder 32–3, 64, 120–2, 137–8; bonds with people 153–5, 157–8; cardiology patient 162–4; cognitively and emotionally impaired youth 98–100; communication differences 126–8; compassion development 123–5; court-ordered therapy 81–2; dementia 104–6; depression 147–8; drug court work 147–8; dying people 92–3, 95–7; earthquake victims 75–6; eating disorder 117–18; fetal alcohol syndrome 109; fire victims 63, 69–71; flood victims 60–1; hospice work 92–4; hysterical student xxiii; incarcerated people 83–5, 89–91; mass shooting victims 63–4, 66–8, 72–4, 77–8, 101–3; mudslide first responders 57–9; nursing home residents 144–5; post-traumatic stress disorder 55–6, 147–8; psychiatric patients 89–91; psychotherapy patient 165–7; school graduation ceremony 112–13; schoolchildren 111–13; sexually abused female 86–8; stress response 66–71; suicidal students 129–30, 157; teletherapy 90, 114–16, 150–2; Veterans 141–2

donkey, and memory care facility resident 20–1

drug court work, and dogs 147–8

dying people, and dogs 92–3, 95–7

earthquake victims, and dogs 75–6

elderly people: dementia, and horses 15–16; dementia, and rabbits 39; nursing home residents, and dogs 145, 159–61; nursing home residents, and rabbits xxi–xxii, 39; Parkinson's disease, and dog 145; stroke patient, and dog 141–2

emotionally abused student, and dog 129

emotionally impaired youth, and dogs 98–100

emus, and abused child 18

equine-assisted learning (EAL) 9–11

equine-assisted therapy (EAP) 15–16

fetal alcohol syndrome 109–10

fire victims, and dogs 63, 69–71

first responders, and dogs: fire 70–1; flood 60; mudslide 57–9

flood victims, and dog 60–1

Forget Me Not Farm 17–19

goats, and abused child 18

guinea pigs: autistic spectrum disorder 43–5; child's confidence building 29–30; psychiatric patient 49–51; teen's relaxation 30–1

heart surgery patient, and dog 162–4

HOPE AACR 63, 66; flood response 60–1; mass shooting response 63–4, 66–8, 72–4; mudslide first responders 57–9; tornado response 55–6

Hope Worldwide 55

horses and ponies: abused child 17, 18; anxious teen 132–4; autism spectrum disorder 6–7; dementia 15–16; equine-assisted learning 9–11; freedom from schedules 3–5; meditation 12–13; suicidal student 130; Sundance Center 9–11

hospice work, and dogs 92–4

hospitals: cancer patient, and dog 96; cardiology patient, and dog 162–4; child patient, and rabbit 46–8; dementia patients, and dog 104–6; suicidal student, and dog 130; Veterans, and dogs 141–2

hysterical student and dog xxiii

incarcerated people, and dogs 83–5, 89–91

insomnia, and dog 129

Kalamazoo mass shooting victims and dogs 101–3

Lowe, Rob 59

mass shooting victims, and dogs 63–4, 66–8, 72–4, 77–8, 101–3
meditation, and horses 12–13
memory care facility resident, and miniature donkey 20–1
mudslide first responders, and dogs 57–9

nursing homes: dogs 144–5, 159–61; rabbits xxi–xxii, 39

office workers, and rabbits 32–4

Parkinson's disease, and dog 145
Pet Partners 49, 92, 162
physically abused children, and dogs 135–6
pigs, and fetal alcohol syndrome 109–10
placebo effect 162, 164
ponies *see* horses and ponies
post-traumatic stress disorder (PTSD): dogs 55–6, 86–8, 129, 147–8; rescued farm animals 23; sexually abused female 86–8; suicidal student 129; tornado victim 55–6
prisoners, and dogs 83–5, 89–91
psychiatric patients: and dogs 89–91, 130; and guinea pig 49–51; suicidal student 130
psychotherapy patient, and dog 165–7

rabbits: blind nursing home resident xxi–xxii; campus pet therapy 40–2; dementia 39; elderly people 38–9; nursing home residents 39; office dynamics 32–3; sensory processing needs 38–9; sick children 46–8
rats, and college students' mood changes 35–7

Sandy Hook mass shooting victims, and dogs 77–8
school refusal, and horse 132–4
schools: autistic child, and guinea pig 43–5; communication differences 126–8; dogs 77–8, 111–13, 126–30; mass shooting victims 77–8; suicidal student 129–30
seniors *see* elderly people
sensory processing needs children and rabbits 38–9
sexual abuse, and dogs 86–8; adopted children 135–6; suicidal student 129
sheep, and at-risk children 23–4
shooting victims, and dogs 63–4, 66–8, 72–4, 77–8, 101–3
Sonoma Mentoring Alliance 23–4
stress: campus pet therapy 41; dogs 66–71, 115; fire victims 69–71; office workers 33; rabbits 33, 41; teletherapy 115; *see also* post-traumatic stress disorder
stroke patient, and dog 141–2
suicidality, and dogs 129–30, 148, 157; eating disorder 117
Sundance Center 9–11

tactility, dementia patients 105
teenagers: anxiety, and horse 132–4; cognitive and emotional impairment, and dogs 98–100; community service, and dog 159, 160; court-ordered therapy, and dogs 81–2; incarceration, and dog 83–5; mass shooting victim, and dog 102; relaxation, and guinea pigs 30–1; school graduation ceremony, and dog 112–13; sexually abused female, and dog 86–8; suicidal student, and dog 129–30
teletherapy, and dogs 90, 114–16, 150–2
therapeutic groups homes, and dog 86–8
therapeutic riding (TR), and autism spectrum disorder 6–7
tornado victim, and dog 55–6

universities and colleges: abused student, and dog 64; anxious and depressed students, and dogs 156–8; campus pet therapy, and rabbit 40–2; hysterical student, and dog xxiii; mass shooting victim, and dog 63–4; students' mood changes, and rats 35–7

Veterans, and dogs 141–2
Virginia Tech mass shooting victim, and dog 63–4

virtual therapy, and dogs 90, 114–16, 150–2

Washington Navy Yard mass shooting victims, and dogs 72–4

Youth Detention Centers, and dog 83–5